DANGEROUS ROAD

The Nuclear Policies of the Obama Administration

Discussions on our nuclear deterrent from

THE CENTER FOR SECURITY POLICY

THE HERITAGE FOUNDATION

THE AMERICAN ENTERPRISE INSTITUTE

THE NEW DETERRENT WORKING GROUP

© 2010 THE CENTER FOR SECURITY POLICY PRESS

WASHINGTON, DC

DANGEROUS ROAD

The Nuclear Policies of the Obama Administration

Ted Bromund ⸱ Lisa Curtis ⸱ Paula DeSutter ⸱ Thomas Donnelly ⸱ Frank J. Gaffney, Jr.

Peter Huessy ⸱ Bruce Klingner ⸱ Walter Lohman ⸱ Adm. James "Ace" Lyons (Ret.)

Vice Adm. Robert Monroe (Ret.) ⸱ Steve Rademaker ⸱ Tom Scheber

Baker Spring ⸱ Congressman Mike Turner ⸱ Amb. Kurt Volker

FRANK J. GAFFNEY, JR.

Publisher

BEN LERNER

Editor-in-Chief

DAVID REABOI

Associate Editor

ISBN 978-0-9822947-3-4

PRINTED IN THE UNITED STATES OF AMERICA

1 2 3 4 5 6 7 8 9 10

FIRST EDITION

THE CENTER FOR SECURITY POLICY
1901 Pennsylvania Avenue, Suite 201
Washington, DC 20006
Phone: (202) 835-9077
Email: info@securefreedom.org

For more information, please see **securefreedom.org**

Contents

Publisher's Note

FRANK J. GAFFNEY, JR.

O n 8 April 2010, President Obama and Russian President Medvedev signed the New Strategic Arms Reduction Treaty, or "New START," promising deep reductions in both parties' strategic nuclear forces. Two days before, the Obama administration unveiled its Nuclear Posture Review, effecting a number of controversial policy and programmatic changes affecting US deterrent strategy and capabilities. And the following week, President Obama hosted the Nuclear Security Summit in Washington, DC, whose stated purpose was to address "the threat of nuclear materials in the hands of terrorists or criminals." Running

Frank J. Gaffney, Jr. is the President and CEO of the Center for Security Policy. Mr. Gaffney formerly acted as the Assistant Secretary of Defense for International Security Policy during the Reagan Administration, following four years of service as the Deputy Assistant Secretary of Defense for Nuclear Forces and Arms Control Policy. Mr. Gaffney is host of Secure Freedom Radio.

through all three was a common leitmotif: Mr. Obama's determination to pursue via exemplary American disarmament initiatives a "world without nuclear weapons."

In response to this frenetic nuclear weapons-related agenda, three different forums were convened by several of the nation's preeminent organizations specializing in security policy. Each featured prominent experts who provided critical assessments and proposed various correctives with respect to the Obama administration's approach to arms control and deterrence. This volume presents the edited transcripts of the following panels' proceedings:

On 6 April 2010, the Heritage Foundation and the American Enterprise Institute jointly convened a two-panel event entitled, "Questioning Obama's Nuclear Agenda—The Conservative Counter-Summit." Both panels were introduced by **Ted Bromund**, the Margaret Thatcher Senior Research Fellow at the Heritage Foundation.

The first panel subject was "How Obama's Nuclear Diplomacy Will Affect America's Allies and Enemies." It was chaired by **Walter Lohman**, Director of the Heritage Foundation's Asian Studies Center, and featured **Amb. Kurt Volker**, former U.S. Ambassador to NATO, as well as **Lisa Curtis** and **Bruce Klingner**, Senior Research Fellows at the Heritage Foundation.

The second panel addressed "The START Follow-On Treaty: The Wrong Approach to Arms Control?" It was chaired by **Baker Spring**, F.M. Kirby Research Fellow in National Security Policy at the Heritage Foundation, and included presentations by **Thomas Donnelly** of the American Enterprise Institute, **Tom Scheber** of the National Institute for Public Policy and **Steve Rademaker**, former U.S. Assistant Secretary of State for International Security and Arms Control.

On 8 April 2010, the Center for Security Policy presented members of the New Deterrent Working Group at the Capitol Visitors Center to discuss the deficiencies of the "New START" treaty, the centrality of a robust American nuclear stockpile and missile defense capability to international stability, the need for a strong strategic "Triad" and related issues. The panel was chaired by **Frank J. Gaffney, Jr.**, President of the Center for Security Policy and former Assistant Secretary of Defense for International Security Policy (Acting). It began with opening remarks by **Rep. Mike**

Turner (R-Ohio), Ranking Member of the Strategic Forces Subcommittee of the House Armed Services Committee and featured: **Paula DeSutter**, former Assistant Secretary of State for Verification and Compliance; **Vice Adm. Robert Monroe**, U.S. Navy, (Ret.), former Director of the Defense Nuclear Agency; **Adm. James "Ace" Lyons**, U.S. Navy (Ret.), former Commander-in-Chief of the U.S. Pacific Fleet; and **Peter Huessy**, President, GeoStrategic Analysis, Inc.

In publishing these panel discussions, we seek to inform the debate about "New START" and other matters of direct relevance to the future adequacy of the US nuclear deterrent. This book provides an urgently needed "second opinion" on the threats facing America—and far more realistic prescriptions for countering them than those on offer from the Obama administration. ▪

Questioning Obama's Nuclear Agenda

A CONSERVATIVE COUNTER-SUMMIT HOSTED BY
THE HERITAGE FOUNDATION AND
THE AMERICAN ENTERPRISE INSTITUTE

TED **BROMUND:** Welcome to the Heritage Foundation and this event on President Obama's Nuclear Agenda, jointly sponsored by Heritage and the American Enterprise Institute.

The coming months will see a flurry of nuclear diplomacy and nuclear strategy. On Thursday, President Obama will sign a Strategic Arms Reduction treaty with Russia in Prague. On April 12th and 13th, the president's nuclear security summit will meet here in Washington, D.C. Right now, the administration is announcing the results of its Nuclear Posture Review, which will determine the future role of nuclear weap-

Introduction by **Ted Bromund**: Margaret Thatcher Senior Fellow, the Heritage Foundation. *This discussion included:* **Walter Loh-man**: Director, Asian Studies Center, the Heritage Foundation; **Amb. Kurt Volker**: former US Ambassador to NATO; **Lisa Curtis**: Senior Research Fellow, the Heritage Foundation; and **Bruce Klingner**: Senior Research Fellow, the Heritage Foundation.

ons in US strategy. Finally, in May, will come the review conference for the nuclear nonproliferation treaty, the NPT. We cannot, of course, address all of these subjects today. After congress reconvenes, our cosponsors, AEI, will host a second event in this series with Senator Kyl as the featured speaker on the legislative prospects for and implications of the president's nuclear diplomacy.

But our point today in our title is that the president's nuclear agenda needs to be seen as a whole. As the president put it in Prague a year ago, he seeks "the peace and security of a world without nuclear weapons." It is in that light that we must understand the events and the activities of the coming weeks and months. In our event today, we'll be focusing on the START-II treaty and on the broader prospects for implications of the president's pursuit of a "world without nuclear weapons." While the START-II treaty promises a brave new world, it is, in many respects, a blast from the past. It hearkens back to the Cold War when the US/Soviet rivalry really did define the world and when a young Barack Obama was writing in a Columbia University magazine in 1983 about his vision for "a nuclear-free world," while condemning discussions of "first- versus second-strike capabilities" that "suit the military-industrial interests" with their "war mentality" and their "billion-dollar erector sets."

More recently, the president has moderated his tone, stating that the US will retain its deterrent capacity as long as any other country holds nuclear weapons. But he continues to believe that movement by the US is central to achieving his overall vision. As he stated last year, "It's naive for us to think that we can grow our nuclear stockpiles. The Russians continue to grow their nuclear stockpiles. And our allies grow their nuclear stockpiles. And that in that environment we're going to be able to pressure countries like Iran and North Korea not to pursue nuclear weapons themselves." I will leave it to our distinguished panelists today to discuss whether it's accurate for the president to imply that the US and its allies have been growing their nuclear stockpiles. What is even less clear is whether the Russians, never mind the Pakistanis, the Indians, the Iranians, or the North Koreans, will be swayed by a US move towards reduced nuclear stockpiles. In 2003, Russian Defense Minister, Sergei Ivanov said, "What we say is one thing. That sounds cynical, but everything that we plan does not necessarily have to be made public. We believe that from the foreign-policy viewpoint it is better to say that. But what we actually do is an entirely different matter if we're talking about nuclear weapons. They are the chief components of our security, and there can be no doubt that attention toward them cannot be relaxed."

But of course, the NPR, the nuclear summit, and the treaty between the US and Russia, are not a matter for the US alone. They obviously concern Russia, for one. They involve nuclear proliferators like Iran and North Korea, who are far more central to today's pressing security challenges than the US and Russian nuclear arsenals. And they involve America's friends and allies around the world, who, for the past sixty years, have lived under the US nuclear shield. The most dangerous possibility is that the president's nuclear agenda will sway none of the world's truly dangerous actors, while at the same time, weakening America's ability to protect and defend its allies, and thereby encouraging them to develop their own nuclear arsenals. In nuclear diplomacy, good intentions are no substitute for an appreciation of the unintended consequences of poorly thought-through arms control.

Now before we begin our first panel, let me make a couple of brief housekeeping notes. We'll have two panels in this series. And in deference to our television audience today, I would ask that members in the audience here please remain seated as we move from panel one to panel two. We will have time for questions after the first panel and after the second panel, and we'll take questions separately for each panel so as to avoid panelists getting up and down. We'll try to end promptly at noon or perhaps just a few minutes thereafter.

Let me first, then, introduce the first panel in our session today, *How President Obama's nuclear diplomacy will affect America's allies and enemies*, moderated by Walter Lohman, the director of the Asian Studies Center at the Heritage Foundation. It features **Ambassador Kurt Volker**, who has been delayed en route, but who informs us he will arrive shortly. Ambassador Volker is a career member of the US Foreign Service and former US Ambassador to NATO. It also features **Lisa Curtis**, Senior Research Fellow at the Asian Studies Center, here at the Heritage Foundation. And **Bruce Klingner**, Senior Research Fellow in Northeast Asia, also my colleague here at the Heritage Foundation. Walter?

WALTER LOHMAN: Thank you, Ted. I think I'll remain seated here to kick things off. I think Ted's laid out very well the agenda this morning, the program. As he says, our job here in the first panel is to explore how President Obama's nuclear diplomacy will be received and how it will impact allies and friends and adversaries and potential adversaries around the world. Forgive us if we prioritize a little bit. We've got a whole forty-five minutes or so to cover the world. It's a big task, but I think we can prioritize well enough.

I spent most of my time here—well, practically all of my time—focused on South and East Asia. I think it's fair to say we've not reached a point where reductions in American and Russian nuclear weapon arsenals are relevant, really, to nuclear powers in Asia. It will have no real impact on any of Asia's nuclear powers: North Korea, China, India, Pakistan. And those are indeed the nuclear powers in the region, fully in compliance with treaty obligations or not. The very idea that reducing our own arms will pressure North Korea, particularly, to cooperate in eliminating its own program is pretty far-fetched, I would say. Likewise, it's hard to imagine that the nuance in our first use policy, that's all over the newspapers this morning—it's hard to imagine that will penetrate the strategic thinking on the Korean peninsula. I really hope that that's not a driver in President Obama's overall approach to nuclear policy. The gap between China and—the Chinese arsenal and the US arsenal—is so great, really, that the Chinese will be able to continue to build and modernize even as we reduce our own deployed weapons and stockpiles for that matter. And India and Pakistan have a unique set of circumstances that drive their own policies as regards nuclear weapons. Pakistan is perhaps the poster child for the topic of the subject next week, the summit next week, which will specifically be on nuclear security. We'll also look at the impact of Obama's policy on allies in Asia, specifically on allies in Asia, particularly Japan, which has, we could call a complicated history with America's nuclear umbrella.

When Ambassador Volker arrives, we can turn to Europe and he can give us some comments on the direct impact, vis-a-vis our friends and allies in Europe. I think he'll also talk briefly about Iran and what we can expect there. Ted has already introduced Bruce and Lisa very briefly. So I don't need to go into much there. Let me just say that we thought, putting together this panel, it would be good to have a couple of Heritage analysts, because they're both people at the top of their fields. Both spent a considerable amount of time in intelligence services. Bruce spent twenty years there. Lisa spent a good portion of the 90s in the intelligence service. She also spent time in Indian and Pakistan in the Foreign Service. So, you know, if somebody else were doing this program, they would likely call Bruce and Lisa over to their facilities to give briefs. So I thought it would be best to make the use of our in-house resource here and have them talk to us. So with that, let me let Lisa start and talk to us about India and Pakistan and reactions there, and likely response to these changes in our nuclear policy. Thank you.

LISA CURTIS: Thanks, Walter. So I'll be talking about South Asia, and how this fits into the Obama administration's nuclear agenda as we understand it at the current time. So the goal of the nuclear security summit is to discuss the prevention of acts of nuclear terrorism and steps that can be taken to secure vulnerable nuclear materials. The summit is indeed part of President Obama's nuclear agenda as laid out in detail on April 5th, 2009. And in that speech, he put forward the broad objectives of reducing the number of nuclear weapons systems in the world and reducing the likelihood of their use. As well as reducing or eliminating the process of any further nuclear testing, stopping further production of nuclear materials that could be used directly to make weapons, and strengthening the rules against the further spread of nuclear weapons capabilities, technologies and materials. And I believe next week's summit will focus both on national measures of the different forty-four countries who are attending as well as an international framework to enhance nuclear security. But I believe the actual movement on President Obama's nuclear agenda is directly linked to the geo-security dynamics in the various regions of the world as well as military balance questions among regional rivals. And nowhere are these regional dynamics more complex than in South Asia. Perhaps even more complex than the transport arrangements we're going to experience next week because of the nuclear security summit.

Now of course, both the Indian and Pakistani prime ministers will be attending the summit. But the reality is reducing global nuclear dangers requires persistent and multifaceted regional engagement. Simply put, India's decision-making on nuclear issues is inherently linked to what China does as well as Pakistan, while Pakistani decisions are directly linked to Indian actions. Thus, addressing the regional security dynamics between these three nuclear armed states is essential when we talk about reducing global nuclear dangers. I'm not going to go into the details of the regional tensions, but suffice it to say that this period is not a particularly auspicious one when it comes to Indo-Pakistani relations as well as Indian-Chinese relations. But that said, past agreements between India and Pakistan on nuclear issues, particularly the 1999 Lahore Declaration, which was developed one year after India and Pakistan conducted back to back nuclear tests, demonstrate it is indeed possible for these two arch rivals to reach nuclear agreements in the absence of comprehensive resolution of all of their disputes. The 1999 Lahore Agreement included commitments to warn each other about missile tests and to place the moratorium on further nuclear testing.

Now let me talk briefly about India. Of course, the biggest development with regard to Indian nuclear issues over the last few years has been the US/India Civil Nuclear Agreement. And this is a deal that will encourage Indian transparency. In fact, it already has by India placing fourteen of its nonmilitary nuclear reactors—its civilian reactors—under IAEA inspections for the first time as well as pressuring it to become more actively involved in strengthening the overall nonproliferation regime. Now the civil nuclear deal has added some complexity to what President Obama is trying to do more broadly on nuclear issues. But I think it still can be argued that the nuclear deal with India will contribute to strengthening efforts to contain nuclear threats since it brings India under the nuclear tent, so to speak. The world's largest democracy and nation that has been a responsible steward of its nuclear weapons and a country whose economic and political clout are undoubtedly growing on the global stage.

Now India rhetorically supports the concept of global zero. And it emphasizes it has always attached the highest importance to the goal of nuclear disarmament. It points to the Rajiv Gandhi Action Plan, which was presented at the Conference on Disarmament in 1988 as a comprehensive initiative on nuclear disarmament. The plan basically calls for a time-bound elimination of nuclear stockpiles and eventually of all nuclear weapons. And India's foreign minister recommitted India to the Gandhi Action Plan just last fall at the United Nations. So India's nuclear doctrine is based on the concept of minimum deterrent. And India also commits itself to a no-first use commitment as part of this doctrine. India refers to itself as a reluctant nuclear power and points to their border war with China in 1962 as the tipping point that convinced Indian leaders it had no choice but to pursue the nuclear option.

And let me briefly touch on Pakistan and its nuclear program. I think the nuclear security question, which will be addressed next week, is particularly salient as Walter mentions, when it comes to Pakistan. Given the current instability there, the AQ Khan debacle, which really was the worst case of nuclear proliferation in history, if we're to sort of talk about its relevance. Now the Obama administration is seeking to reassure Pakistan that the US indeed has no intentions to confiscate Pakistan's nuclear weapons, or to take away its nuclear weapons deterrent. There is a lot of suspicion in the US/Pakistan relationship more broadly, but particularly on the issue of nuclear weapons, you can often find stories about how the US secretly is trying to denude Pakistan of its nuclear weapons capability. So I think there has been an effort to try to reassure Pakistan on this front. Now I think the idea of striking a civil nuclear deal with Pakistan, along the lines of the one that was struck with India, is extremely premature. And I think that message was conveyed to the Pakistani leadership at the strategic dialogue recently at the State Department. I think the A. Q. Khan issue is still fresh in the minds of congressional members. And certainly one of the key tenets to moving forward with the India civil nuclear deal was its solid proliferation record. And Pakistan simply does not have that.

So it was in the mid 1960s, after the Chinese nuclear test in 1964, and Pakistan's calculation that India would also go nuclear that Pakistan decided it would follow in its footsteps. Pakistan's defeat in the 1971 war with India, which resulted in the dismemberment of the country and the establishment of Bangladesh, further convinced then-Pakistan leader Zulfikar Ali Bhutto of Pakistan's need for a nuclear deterrent against India's conventional superiority. So nuclear decision-making in Pakistan is clearly under the control of the military. Pakistan does not have a no-first-use doctrine and maintains that India's conventional superiority necessitates this doctrine. When President Zardari posited the idea of implementing a no first use doctrine in 2008, shortly after coming to power, the military quickly reined him in from this position.

So let's get back to the nuclear security issue. There's been a lot of media hype on this issue, particularly with the instability we've seen in Pakistan, the uptick in terrorist attacks: three thousand Pakistanis were killed in terrorist attacks in 2009. So there is certainly reason to think about these issues. But I think there has been a bit of hype surrounding the issue as well. I would say the probability of Taliban militants overrunning the country and somehow gaining control of Pakistani nuclear weapons is fairly far-fetched. The real danger lies in a scenario of al-Qaeda or Taliban-linked militants using links that they might have to some retired military or intelligence officials or nuclear scientists, to infiltrate the system, slowly and gradually. And that is the issue that we need to guard against. And I think we've even seen, through the case of 2001, where a couple of former Pakistani nuclear scientists actually met with Osama bin Laden in August of 2001.

Former DCI George Tenet has written about this in his memoirs. He writes about how he informed Musharraf about the meeting, encouraging Pakistan to take steps. And this actually prompted the nuclear security program that the US has with Pakistan now. This is the one hundred million that's been invested over the last several years in helping Pakistan establish permissive action links as well as personnel reliability programs to ensure the safety and security of its nuclear assets. So I think the key here is that having a trusting, robust partnership with Pakistan is really the best way to encourage the safety and security of Pakistan's nuclear weapons. I'm going to stop there. I've given enough background. But I would look forward to any questions you might have.

BRUCE KLINGNER: Well, since Ted already used one of the quotes I was going to start with from President Obama, and Walter already made a number of my points on North Korea, I'm tempted to declare my job done and just move straight to Q and A, but let me continue a little bit. Just to reemphasize one of the points that President Obama has made is that it would be difficult to pressure North Korea and Iran to give up their nuclear weapons as long as the US and Russia as well as US allies continue to build up.

So that conversely one would presume that North Korea and Iran would be more likely to denuclearize if the US and Russia reduced their own nuclear stockpiles. Well, apparently Pyongyang and Tehran didn't get the memo because they've continued their longtime pursuit of nuclear weapons even during the past several decades as the US and Russia were reducing their nuclear arsenals. North Korean and Iranian calculation on developing nuclear weapons and proliferating nuclear technology were irrespective of the number of weapons that the US and Russia and others had.

So therefore, in an Asian context, the START treaty and the quest for a nuclear-free world did nothing to curtail Pyongyang's and Tehran's nuclear aspirations, nor prevent nuclear proliferation. Indeed, the lack of US nuclear testing did not prevent North Korea from exploding nuclear devices in both 2006 and 2009.

Now as we look back a year ago, even as the president was approaching the podium to give his speech at Prague, the real world intruded, because North Korea had violated UN resolutions by launching a long-range missile. And that, of course, was followed a month later by a nuclear test. So one wonders if someone had to hand the president a post-it note to stick on the text of his Prague speech so that he would include a statement such as "we need real and immediate consequences for countries caught breaking the rules or trying to leave the treaty without cause."

It was a case of the here and now weighing down the more lofty objective of the Prague speech. As he emphasized, "rules must be binding, violations must be punished, words must mean something. The world must stand together to prevent the spread of these weapons. Now is the time for strong international response."

In another forum, we could debate whether the current policy of strategic patience is sufficient to get North Korea to give up their nuclear weapons. But if we look back even a little bit further to last January upon inauguration, there were the euphoric expectations that the change in US leadership, the new administration's willingness to engage, even pledges to seek summits without preconditions with rogue nations, would bring about hoped-for breakthroughs.

But, to be sure, getting North Korea and Iran to give up their nuclear weapons programs will be extremely difficult, if not impossible. Following a series of North Korean provocations and violations of UN resolutions last year, the Obama administration reversed course and implemented a two track approach of both pressure and negotiation with North Korea.

We believe this is a proper approach and one, indeed, that the Heritage Foundation has advocated for three years.

But to emphasize, again, the difficulties truly getting to zero, North Korea's belligerent behavior last year created a belated dawning realization that North Korea has spent forty years developing a nuclear weapons program and not a bargaining chip. And that it created a much greater sense of pessimism in Washington, both within the administration and among outside experts, that engagement would work and that denuclearization was possible with North Korea.

One thing that Obama's quest for zero does is provide North Korea some political cover for maintaining its own nuclear weapons. We saw in September 2009, that North Korea now is declaring that denuclearization of the Korean peninsula is only in the context of a global effort to build a world free of nuclear weapons. So we now see that Pyongyang is tying its own denuclearization, which was required under a number of previous commitments, to worldwide US disarmament. Its a new demand beyond the previous parameters of the six party talks.

Now turning to US allies in Asia, if the Prague speech and the quest for zero didn't have an impact on rogue nations, it appears to have had some impact on our allies in Asia. South Korea sought specific inclusion of a written guarantee of the US nuclear umbrella (extended deterrence) during last year's bilateral summit between President Lee Myung-bak and President Obama. But even having included that written guarantee of our commitment, Seoul continues to remain suspicious of the US resolve to continue insisting on North Korea denuclearization. Because it fears that Washington will instead settle merely for containment. Seoul is also nervous about the US commitment to defend South Korea, including the continued viability of the US nuclear umbrella.

Now, in Japan, the Prague speech of President Obama encouraged the new DPJ-led government to advocate the US adopt a 'no first use' pledge as well as implement a Northeast Asian nuclear free zone. The DPJ sees these objectives as consistent with Japan's long-standing three 'nuclear no's' policy. Now conversely, privately, South Korean officials expressed concern that these Japanese objectives would undermine US extended deterrence in the region.

The DPJ pursues these nuclear-free goals even as it continues its contradictory policy of embracing US nuclear weapons as part of its own security strategy. But it has failed to see that embracing the first part of that strategy undermines the second part. Yet successive Japanese leaders, including the current Hatoyama administration, have denied any inherent contradiction.

The arms control focus has been predominately on the US and Russia and more recently rogue nations. But there is another important player, another nuclear power in Northeast Asia which is, of course, China. It's useful to realize that Beijing views nuclear deterrence very differently from the United States. Chinese military writings indicate that the term for deterrence actually incorporates strong elements of coercion and intimidation as well.

Chinese military writings indicate that the purpose of deterrence is to "halt or prevent the other side from starting a conflict, and thus protect one's own interests from aggression." This is very similar to the Western view. But it also reveals that Chinese strategy is to "shake the other side's will to resist and thus seize those interests or benefits that originally would have required conflict in order to obtain them."

According to the People's Liberation Army encyclopedia, the strategy of deterrence involves the "display of military power or the threat of the use of military power in order to compel an opponent to bow." In other words, Chinese strategists see deterrence as providing the means to achieve one's own strategic goals and defeat an enemy without having to resort to the actual use of force.

So not only can a defending side utilize deterrence to compel an aggressor to abandon offensive intentions, as the US believes, but an offensive side can also implement strategic deterrence, causing a defender to conclude that the cost of resistance is too high. One can't help but think of the case of Taiwan.

By causing the other side to capitulate without fighting, or with minimal violence, then one can achieve the goal of not fighting yet causing the enemy's troops to surrender. This, of course, is very consistent with the Chinese strategist Sun-Tzu's observation that the greatest general is the one who can win without fighting. So I'll stop there and look forward to your questions.

WALTER LOHMAN: Kurt, do you want to take the microphone? You missed all of the flowery introductions and that sort of thing. But the one thing I did want to note on your resume, the thing that popped out to me, is you served with Senator McCain. As an alumni myself, alumnus myself of Senator McCain, it's good to have you here.

KURT VOLKER: Yeah, thanks, Walter. And I apologize for being late. I misestimated the transit here. But I did want to—maybe it's good that we heard about some of the Asian proliferation perspectives first, because I'll circle back now and talk about broader nuclear policy issues, a bit about Russia, a bit about allies, and then a bit about nonproliferation.

I started—I studied in graduate school in the early 1980s and did a lot of work at that time on strategic nuclear issues. That was the thing of the day. And then joined the Foreign Service in 1988 and saw the Berlin Wall come down a year later and then saw the Soviet Union dissolve two years after that. And I didn't think I'd ever be talking about SLBMs and ICBMs and counting rules and all that stuff ever again. But here we are.

And I think that says a couple of things about some of the surprising ways the world has changed since the fall of the Soviet Union. There are— on the current agenda, there are a lot of things out there.

Today, the administration is announcing its Nuclear Posture Review. We have the START treaty teed up to be signed in Prague next week. We have the nuclear summit that the administration is convening here in Washington the week after that. Or I guess about ten days from now. And we have the NPT review conference and the efforts at restraint and non-proliferation efforts there.

This set of issues and these things that are brought up by this calendar are, in my view, in many ways separate issues. They're related, but you have to actually look at them a little distinctly to understand how they fit together. And so I'll take them a little bit sequentially and bring in some of the other issues about outlines in Russia and so forth along the way.

First off, the START treaty, to take that, what this is about is basically putting a framework around the strategic nuclear arsenals of the US and Russia. So we're talking about ICBMs, submarine launch ballistic missiles, bombers, and meeting residual high numbers. So fifteen hundred and fifty, the US and Russia on the strategic side. I think it's hard to complain about that. It puts a framework around it. It gives us a significant number of strategic nuclear weapons in order to carry out deterrence. We'll see the details, but it includes a verification and inspection regime. So this seems like a useful thing to do.

A colleague of mine, Kori Schake, wrote an excellent piece for ForeignPolicy.com, which I refer you to if you're interested. She actually points out, this could even result in an increase in actual nuclear warheads, given the counting rules. I'm not sure that it will. It really depends on how people apply it. But I think, at least as a step, having this framework is a useful thing to do.

But it then begs a lot of other questions. The first question it begs, in my mind, is non-strategic nuclear weapons. So: tactical nuclear weapons. Here, the United States and NATO have reduced dramatically the number of tactical nuclear weapons that we have in Europe over the past two decades—I think it's a ninety percent-plus reduction. Whereas we see that Russia continues to have over five thousand tactical nuclear warheads, most of them very close to Europe, rather than very close to China.

So I think that is an area that is immediately exposed by the framework around the strategic: Well, what happens to all of these Russian tactical nuclear weapons? When you look at the numbers again, fifteen hundred or so strategic, but dwarfed by five thousand plus tactical nuclear weapons. And the difference between tactical and nuclear doesn't really matter if you're the recipient. It and the terminology only means distance. So if you're in Russia and you're in Europe, then it's the same thing. So I think that is an area that should be immediately up for discussion.

How do we get Russia to reduce this grotesque number of tactical nuclear weapons that they have very close to Europe? Russia's answer to that is troubling. Russia's military doctrine has been to increase its reliance on nuclear weapons as its conventional forces are weak, rather than to decrease reliance on nuclear weapons.

And it's also said that it's not going to do anything about tactical nuclear weapons as long as the US maintains *any* tactical nuclear weapons in Europe. Which means it's insisting on a de-coupling, a nuclear de-coupling, of the United States and Europe before it would even consider doing anything on its tactical nuclear weapons. So that's a very troubling situation.

I don't—so, again, I don't see a problem with putting a framework around the strategic nuclear weapons where we're putting it. But I do see a problem with the state of play on tactical nuclear weapons and it's principally a problem in how Russia's approaching it. And I think we have to focus on that. Focusing on our own tactical nuclear weapons, which are miniscule in number compared to where they were or compared to where Russia has them, I think is the wrong starting point. I think we really need to look at what Russia's doctrine is. And what Russia's nuclear posture itself is.

Those sets of issues also, I should say, bring in immediately the role of allies. And that is something that has been rather absent from the discussion thus far about the START treaty and about the nuclear issue globally is, well, what about France and the UK, which have their own nuclear deterrent forces? And what about the role of NATO? And here I think as I understand what will be announced today—it will actually say that the US is not going to propose anything else beyond the START treaty without talking to allies and I think that's the right answer. I think we do have to talk to allies about it. And I know from my own conversations that the French and also the British—if we have a new government in Britain in a month—even more so the Tory government, are going to be very concerned about further steps on nuclear weapons of which they are not a full participant in the decision-making because it directly affects their own nuclear deterrent postures.

Then that gets to the question about, well, how does this affect the question of rogue states? When you talk about nonproliferation, there are really two sides to the coin. One of them is a nonproliferation regime for countries that want to play by the rules. And it's good to have those rules, and it's good to try to enforce, and it's good to try to use those rules to minimize the proliferation that does go on.

But we also have to be very realistic. There are some countries who deliberately, intentionally, are seeking nuclear weapons in violation of the rules, and find it actually may be an advantageous position from their point of view, to have these rules in place to hold back everybody else while they go forward. And that requires a different kind of approach in dealing with proliferation. So you've got to have your NPT regime strengthening. And I'm glad to see that that will be a focus of discussion in the coming month.

But it can't stop there. Everything we've done thus far on Iran and North Korea has been unsuccessful. And I think that applies to both the Obama and the Bush administrations. You can't look back on the last ten years and think that we've done well on dealing with rogue states acquiring nuclear weapons. They've actually done a good job in acquiring them, and not shown any degree of being deterred from seeking the nuclear weapons. Which comes back to the role of nuclear weapons. In an environment where some states will be seeking to acquire them, I think it is important to emphasize the role of nuclear weapons in deterrence. It is important for countries such as the United States to maintain a strong nuclear capability so that a proliferating state will know that no matter what it does, they're still going to have a vulnerable position vis-a-vis the United States or other major nuclear powers, and I think it's very important to have that very clear.

The other thing that it emphasizes is if they are not deterred in seeking weapons, can we be *sure* that they would be deterred in using them? And the answer is no. I don't think we can be *sure*. We can do everything we can to increase the pain involved of any nuclear use by those countries, but we can't be sure.

Which also emphasizes the role and the need for missile defense. Here I think—if I understand the result of the negotiations correctly, I think the administration did the right thing by avoiding any linkage between strategic nuclear reductions and strategic nuclear limitations and development of missiles defenses. Both the Bush administration and the Obama administration have pursued missile defenses based in Europe to protect against the risk of an Iranian nuclear weapon. And I think that is the right thing to do and a necessary thing to do in a world where you have rogue states that take advantage of a nonproliferation regime, rather than abide by it.

And then a final point that I would make, when you walk through that set of issues, is that you have to think of nuclear weapons not only as reducing the risk of their use as a goal, but remember that we have another goal, which is, we want to live in a prosperous, safe, and more democratic world. One that is respectful of human rights, one that's respectful of the rights of democracies, one that is generally good for our kind of society in the world. By talking only about the use or non-use or the limitations on nuclear weapons, we're missing a big part of the strategic picture of what we should care about as a country.

We need to look at that also in tandem with, well, how is that going to shape the development of the world? And if you have countries like an Iran with a brutal religious authoritarian regime, that supports terrorist groups like Hezbollah and Hamas, that threatens to destroy Israel, that plays a very dangerous regional role, if you have a country like North Korea which is one of the most brutal in oppressing its own population, you have to say, okay, we need to look at nuclear weapons, but we also need to look at the kinds of regimes that we're dealing with, the role that they play, and we need to be thinking about how our capacities, including a nuclear capacity as a deterrent, need to be applied as a means of political force in order to try to affect the development in the world in a more positive direction.

I think if we talk only about nuclear limitations and drive towards a global zero, which, you know, is a wonderful goal like reducing poverty or, you know, reducing—or living in a world without war—the reality of the world that we live in today means we're going to have nuclear weapons. We ought to have nuclear weapons in order to protect ourselves, our allies, and also to try to shape the development of the world in a more positive direction for the long term. So those would be some of the points of context that I would put around a lot of the debate here and maybe tying together some of the Russia issues, the ally issues, and the regional issues.

WALTER LOHMAN: Great. Thank you, thank you. We'll open it up for questions. We have time for two or three. Yes, ma'am. Right here in the white shirt.

QUESTIONER: Some experts say that when Obama's administration is speaking about START, about nonproliferation, Russia is increasing its sphere of influence and an example is the Ukraine. And it's now to be a member of NATO. Do you think so?

KURT VOLKER: Sure. Well, I would say—I think that's exactly what Russia is doing. Russia is both negotiating a strategic arms limitations treaty with us, and they wanted to squeeze out of it what they could, as any negotiator would. But at the end of the day, it's useful for them to have a framework around these things. But that has no bearing whatsoever on their desire to re-establish a sphere of influence around themselves in Central and Eastern Europe. And they're very busily going about that.

And you didn't mention Abkhazia and South Ossetia, but you may as well have done. Also Ukraine. Also using their strategic industries, such as energy, all for that purpose.

I think it's important that we do two things as the United States. One of them is we reject explicitly the idea that there should be any sphere of influence in Europe. Every country in Europe has a right to its independence and sovereignty and we should be on the side of those who are supporting independence and sovereignty of every European state. We should be doing what we can to help them in that respect also, through our Freedom of Support Act assistance, for example. Through non-recognition of the breakaway republics of Abkhazia and South Ossetia. And through continued efforts to strengthen democratic institutions in Ukraine and Georgia and Armenia and Azerbaijan and so on. And through putting pressure on resolving regional conflicts. Whether it is the Geneva process for Abkhazia and South Ossetia or whether it's the Minsk group for Ngorno-Karabakh, we should be on the side of pushing to say that we want to see these things resolved. So that's one thing that we should be doing.

The other thing that we should be doing is making clear that we believe in a better vision. We don't see a zero sum between Russia's sphere of influence and a US or a Western sphere of influence. We believe in values. We believe that societies that are based on democracy and market economy, rule of law, human rights, are fundamentally good for their own people and good for the world that we live in. We don't see a trade-off between countries like Georgia that are building institutions and developing the realization of those values in their own countries and any kind of threat to anybody else, and we would urge that Russia similarly look at the world as one where there could be a common good rather than a zero sum.

QUESTIONER: Stuart Ritter, a retired nuclear submarine officer that may be the only person in the room who's ever seen or touched a nuclear weapon, or controlled them. I'm concerned about the piece that says the Russians think that this treaty will limit missile defense and our saying that it won't. That has got to be resolved before the Senate can ever take a look at this thing and not have it be a set of handcuffs in one direction. Would the panel want to comment on that controversy?

KURT VOLKER: Well, first off, the premise you're making is one I agree with. That this treaty should not in any way limit the ability to pull in missile defenses. I think we then need to see the language that comes out in the treaty. What I understand is that there may be a reference to missile defenses, in a relationship between strategic nuclear issues—strategic nuclear offensive and strategic defensive capability—in the preamble. But nothing limiting in the treaty itself. So we need to see what the exact language is. And I think we need to be very clear, as you indicate in your question, that we cannot be in a position where the fact of a strategic--a limitation on strategic offensive arms—which we agree with, would in any way be construed as requiring a limitation on missile defenses, because those are critical for defending ourselves against countries like Korea or Iran or others.

WALTER LOHMAN: If I could just change the subject briefly to South Asia. You know, the first two questions were about the meat of the issue, which is Russia and the US. In particular, regarding India, India has sort of a carve-out in the international system. Right? I mean, that's what the nuclear agreement was all about, was getting them a carve-out. They're responsible stewards of their nuclear arsenal, etc. And so we had created a way that they could pursue their nuclear programs, civilian nuclear programs, to the full extent of international law without signing up to some of the things that others are signed up to, that are referenced in all of these efforts by President Obama. How do you think the Indians are seeing this? I mean, is their special carve-out under some sort of long-term threat by— involving a network of new programs and new agreements, arrangements, etc.?

LISA CURTIS: Well, I think India would prefer that the discussions next week focus on the nuclear safety and security issue. And, as Ambassador Volker was pointing out, these are all nuclear-related issues, the START treaty, the Nuclear Posture Review, the nuclear security summit, but they're also very distinct in many different ways. So the nuclear security summit, I think India will be looking at that to focus really on nuclear security—securing vulnerable nuclear materials. Whatever states can do individually, but also maybe developing some kind of international framework, I think that's what we're looking at in terms of the nuclear security summit.

If you're looking more broadly at the civil nuclear deal, we've been through sort of the hashing and rehashing of what that deal did for the nuclear nonproliferation treaty and the overall rules and regulations framework. And certainly it makes it more complex where you have an overall global effort to restrict nuclear reprocessing because of the fact that it can be used in a nuclear weapons program, and then we just signed a reprocessing agreement with India to complete the civil nuclear deal.

So certainly there are some complex issues there, but I think you hit the nail on the head. It's not a black and white system here. And India has its security concerns. I think it was very important that India did have a solid proliferation record. And that is what influenced the decision to move forward with the civil nuclear deal, of course initiated by the Bush administration, but continued by the Obama administration.

BRUCE KLINGNER: Just to add on missile defense, though I think the second panel's going to get into it more deeply, but my understanding is the discussion of the missile defense was put in the prelude to the treaty so that you can 'agree to disagree.' When I was a member of the Conventional Armed Forces in Europe Treaty delegation in Europe during the Soviet era, that's what we would do. If we couldn't agree on a certain issue, in order to maintain progress, we would put it in the prelude. That way each side can claim its own interpretation was correct.

But the importance of missile defense was emphasized when North Korea launched its long-range missile back in April 2009. We could stand on the shores of Hawaii or California, holding up the UN resolution, saying, you're not supposed to be doing this. And yet they did. We all had some greater degree of comfort, knowing that we had a missile defense system that was active off of Hawaii, that was based in Alaska. That, had it been a launch during a time of crisis or time of tension, at least we would have had a sense that we could deal with the North Korean nuclear or missile threat at the time. So clearly, missile defense is something that we need to maintain even as everyone strives to reduce nuclear weapons.

QUESTIONER: Yeah, thank you. Sean Handen with AFP. I wanted to focus on Asia a little bit. Isn't there the potential that actually this stance could be welcomed by some US allies? Particularly Japan, India, if you call it an ally, I mean, India, as you mentioned, has the—India has now first use, Japan, of course, has advocated against nuclear weapons. Australia, for that matter. Or, for mere perspective, would this be—more be a rhetorical stance by these countries rather than a—rather than an actual look at their security?

BRUCE KLINGNER: Well, on Japan, it's a contradictory policy. They embrace the three "nuclear no's" and a nuclear free world. And Foreign Minister Okada has pressed for nuclear free zones, no first use, etc. Yet at the same time, Japan remains very reliant on nuclear weapons—the US's. They continue to rely on the US nuclear umbrella and do not want a degradation in that capability in order to maintain their security. So, it is an inherently contradictory policy. Though successive administrations, including the current one, feel that there is no contradiction. So it is rhetorically embracing the goals of the Prague speech but, in reality, wanting to maintain the US nuclear umbrella, because Japan is in the shadow of the North Korean nuclear threat. They've been overflown by North Korean missiles several times.

LISA CURTIS: On India, I would put India as cautiously supportive. They repeat the Gandhi Action Plan that they proposed back in 1988 for global nuclear disarmament and they're kind of reiterating or reemphasizing that, "look, we've been saying this for the past twenty years." But it is—I think it is more rhetorical. When you get down to it, India is judging what it's doing with its nuclear weapons based on the regional realities that it faces. And so I think that, whereas rhetorically there can be some agreement, when it gets down to it, it's going to take some kind of multifaceted regional engagement to deal with the nuclear dangers in the subcontinent. Moreso than what's been done between Russia and the US with START.

WALTER LOHMAN: And I hope we don't get in a situation where the US is the only one more than rhetorically committed to this whole idea. Last question here.

QUESTIONER: I want to ask about North Korea. Mr. Klingner had mentioned earlier that--the two track approach… has been going, [but] there is no progress that has been made. And actually the level of the threat has grown. Because North Korea tested its second nuclear missile test, so I want to ask your suggestion. How we make progress on this problem of [the North Korean] nuclear program?

BRUCE KLINGNER: We, we could have a whole panel on that. But just sort of, very succinctly, people now realize that the unrealistic expectations of last year have died, and that North Korea has long been the problem rather than the successive US policies towards North Korea. But, even as we utilize a two track approach of using pressure and negotiation, they're two sides of the same coin. And we do need that third track of sufficient defense in case all else goes wrong.

But as we try to move forward with North Korea, a policy of more pain and more gain may be effective. We need to plug the loopholes of the current UN resolution. And also we need to go after the other end of the proliferation pipeline. The US and the UN have been reluctant to identify those other nations which have been violating UN resolution 1874 and the predecessors. Syria, Iran, Burma come to mind. So we need to identify those.

We also need to resume enforcing international law against North Korean illicit activities. And we also need to identify if there are other governments or companies or banks that are complicit in either the inflow or outflow of North Korea nuclear and missile technology. But also there can be a strategic blueprint offering greater gains for North Korea if they return to their denuclearization pledge. You can add lanes in the road of engagement. You can not only focus on nuclear, but you can expand it to missile, humanitarian and developmental assistance, though they need to remain under the precepts of transparency and reciprocity and conditionality. So we could go into more detail, but I'll leave it at that.

WALTER LOHMAN: Great. Well, thank you--thank you all. And thanks to our panelists for joining us and offering your expertise. ▪

The START Follow-On Treaty: The Wrong Approach to Arms Control?

A CONSERVATIVE COUNTER-SUMMIT HOSTED BY
THE HERITAGE FOUNDATION AND
THE AMERICAN ENTERPRISE INSTITUTE

TED BROMUND: Our second panel of the day is *The START Follow On Treaty: The Wrong Approach To Arms Control?* This panel will be moderated by my colleague here at the Heritage Foundation, **Baker Spring**, the F. M. Kirby Research Fellow in National Security Policy. The panel also features, going from Baker's left to right, **Thomas Donnelly**, the Director of the Center for Defense Studies at the American Enterprise Institute. AEI, for those of you who were not here for the first panel this morning is our cosponsor in this two panel event. And AEI will be reciprocating with a cosponsored AEI/Heritage panel when Congress reconvenes.

Introduction by **Ted Bromund**: Margaret Thatcher Senior Fellow, the Heritage Foundation. *This panel included:* **Baker Spring**: FM Kirby Research Fellow in National Security Policy, the Heritage Foundation; **Thomas Donnelly**, Resident Fellow and Director, Center for Defense Studies, the American Enterprise Institute; **Thomas Scheber**, Vice President, National Institute for Public Policy; and **Steve Rademaker**, former US Assistant Secretary of State for International Security and Arms Control.

They will be announcing that separately. Our second panelist, **Tom Scheber,** Vice President at the National Institute for Public Policy. And **Stephen Rademaker**, Senior Counsel, BGR Government Affairs and former US Assistant Secretary of State for International Security and Arms Control. Thank you. Baker?

BAKER SPRING: Thank you. As moderator of this panel, I think that it's appropriate for me to compare what this panel will be addressing to the earlier one. What you saw with the earlier one was the question of: what's the international lay of the land? What are the international perspectives on the questions that the Obama administration is clearly wrestling with now? The future of the US nuclear arsenal, its broader strategic posture, nonproliferation issues and arms control.

What this panel will do, I hope, is provide you what I would describe as the inside-out perspective that is from the US program, US defense budgets, US arms control and nonproliferation initiatives, as whether they meet the security needs of the country and for that matter US allies as we are looking out.

I think that there are three issues that the Obama administration needs to address here, both with regard to the nuclear posture in particular, as well as the broader strategic posture. One is: does it meet the requirement of today's and tomorrow's security, given a dramatic change in the international security structure, following the end of the Cold War and the collapse of the Soviet Union? To me, that is the broadest question and that is one where I think that Tom Donnelly has some really unique perspective on—I look forward to hearing it and I think that you will as well.

The second is what's going on in the nonproliferation and arms control fields—clearly that is a very key interest for the Obama administration and I think it goes right up to the top, that the president has taken a personal interest in this. The question is, are they sound? Are they sound with regard to the relationship that the United States has with other countries in the world, whether that be a friendlier ally relationship or one that's more adversarial in nature? Arms control is going to clearly play a role in where it fits in, in terms of the future agenda for the administration and as Congress looks on that agenda. I think that Steve Rademaker is uniquely qualified to comment, given his experience both within Congress and the executive branch on these issues.

The final is, what's--what are the key components of the strategic posture of the United States and, again, more specifically in today's context of the nuclear element of that? Tom Scheber of the National Institute for Public Policy has very deep experience with regard to nuclear planning issues and strategic posture planning issues. The programmatics involved with that, the governing policies. And that's in the office of the Secretary of Defense as well as in the Navy. So those are the perspectives that I think that he will provide and he provided keen insights on these issues as a supporting staff member to the Strategic Posture Commission, which I think made a strong set of recommendations regarding these issues, most broadly speaking. So with that, I'll turn it over to Tom Donnelly.

THOMAS DONNELLY: Thanks, Baker. I also want to say thanks to everybody at Heritage for trying to throw together this home and away series of conferences that we're going to have. We're very pleased to be doing that with you and we're just kind of waiting for Congress to return and particularly the Senate to figure out what it thinks about not only the treaty, but the Nuclear Posture Review and whatever may come out of the nuclear summit next week other than some massive traffic jams for those of us who live in Washington or nearby. And that's really where I'd like to start.

I am not a nuclear expert, really, by past experience or trade. But I do think the moment that we're in or fast approaching is really a moment where it's appropriate to take a step back and look more broadly at how the tools of arms control and our nuclear arsenal fit more broadly as tools of statecraft into the broader picture of American strategy because, obviously, the world is changing, international politics are changing, the military affairs are undergoing profound changes. And I would argue that the Obama administration, not being the look forward that it's advertised as, is really a very much rear view mirror, Cold War framework for considering both the question of arms control--it's notable that this is a bilateral treaty agreed with the former Soviet Union or the rump thereof. And the things that I would certainly worry about going forward would include Russia, both as an international and political actor and as a nuclear power, but the panoply of rising powers, declining powers, dangerous powers, unstable powers—and particularly those armed with a variety of nuclear capabilities—is really metastasizing quite rapidly.

So if we're bidding goodbye to a bilateral balance of terror, we're looking forward to a much more complex and I would say dangerous multipolar, not only collection of rogue states or small nuclear powers, but a quite different potential nuclear great power balance. And I'm much more concerned about whether the regime that we're about to consider really opens up an opportunity, say, for the Chinese who are modernizing and expanding their arsenals to try to take a step that they can certainly afford to become a nuclear power at the level of United States or Russia.

Now we don't know what exactly that would mean, either for the spread of Chinese geopolitical influence or what it would do to intimidate or worry our allies not only in East Asia, but in South Asia and in Central Asia and indeed globally. But that's exactly the point. We don't understand what this world will look like in any great detail or what the implications of these changes would be. And therefore it seems much more, you know, prudent, not to say conservative with a small "c," to essentially adopt the approach that every physician adopts when he works on a patient, and that is "first, do no harm."

And it's not clear that the numbers and particularly the decision to at least postpone if not really end American nuclear modernization efforts is sort of, limp and pathetic as they were, or as drawn-out as they were, is going to prepare us better or make us, or put us more at the mercy of events going forward. And again, I don't propose to have precise answers or specific answers to these. I think it might be possible to live, for example, within the numbers that are contained in the START treaty. Or the proposed START treaty.

But that would depend upon a vigorous program of modernization, because the combination of reducing the arsenal we have and producing and, pardon me, retaining, and simply extending the life of the arsenal that we have, which is wildly inappropriate for the world that we face, which is very much a Cold War legacy of launchers or delivery systems that carry multiple, many multiple warheads. And with warheads themselves that are much more destructive than one would want to have going forward, really puts us at a hamstrung position or threatens to put us in a hamstrung position for the world that we can see pretty clearly coming down the road. Certainly within the time horizon that the treaty will take effect and the decisions about modernization will play out. Because these are really much longer term decisions that ought to be, I would argue, considered at much greater length, debated more openly and more fully and not just embraced because of a vague sense that we need to move toward a world free of nuclear weapons.

The world of nuclear weapons over the past fifty years, we should never forget initiated by ourselves, in response to a very unpleasant and unpalatable set of, if you will, conventional choices that President Truman faced in 1945. So we already know there are conditions under which using nuclear weapons appears to an American president to be not the worst choice that he faces. And we would be just ahistorical and forgetful if we didn't recall what the parameters of those decisions, that decision was, and just to say, "well, that could never happen again," that we would never find ourselves in a similar situation where we might want to at least have the choice of doing so.

And in this regard, it's worth remembering that in 1991, prior to the beginning of Operation Desert Storm, Secretary of State James Baker met with Tariq Aziz, his opposite member in Baghdad and said "it would be really a shame if you Iraqis employed chemical or biological weapons on American forces deployed in the Gulf," the implication being very strong and very clear—as Secretary Baker wrote in his memoirs, the Bush administration, the then-George H. W. Bush administration, retained the possibility, or at least the threat, of employing nuclear weapons, and the line used by Secretary Baker was that the use of chemical or biological weapons against American troops would make the American people cry out for revenge.

Now whether that was, in fact, a reflection of policies that were being, whether there was never, say a military plan for employing tactical nuclear weapons in Operation Desert Storm. Nonetheless, it was a serious threat. It was taken seriously by the Iraqis. And, in fact, sort of contrary to many people's expectations, in the conduct of Desert Storm, the Iraqis did not employ certainly the chemical weapons that they had in large stockpiles which they had pushed forward and could have used, certainly had the capability to use.

So again, we should remember that the world has been much more complex. The nuclear weapons, for all their terrors, have contributed to American security for a long time and in many ways. And to just say, ipso facto, or to even suggest, because in all this rhetoric, there's always at least very small—and you have to be a sort of a scholastic philosopher to tease out exactly what the language that the Nuclear Posture Review contains—might actually mean. But at any rate, certainly the larger picture is of an American president, quite clearly renouncing a past effective tool of American strategy and moving forward, essentially, to create quite different security and strategic conditions, under which it's reasonable to ask whether the United States will be able to secure its interests in a world that's changing quite rapidly and in particular in which there is a narrative of American decline and the rise of the rest.

So assuming that American military preeminence is a given going forward, it seems to me like a very debatable proposition and one that ought to be debated before we sign a treaty that will have consequences not only for our relations with Russia, but with our posture and our relations and our security guarantees to allies and friends around the world. And in particular, if we intend to extend deterrence, as Secretary Clinton has suggested, to imply a nuclear umbrella, in places such as the Persian Gulf where we haven't had to make that kind of guarantee or even suggest that we would make that kind of guarantee before, then again, we should adopt this approach of thinking before signing. And thinking before making budgetary and programmatic decisions that will have long term effects and that can only be questioned in the minds of both our friends and our enemies and our possible adversaries going forward. And fit into a larger context of American strategy and American posture that this administration has, by its actions, called into question. And that the START treaty, the posture review, and probably the summit that we'll see next week, is more likely to raise further questions than to answer the questions that have already been laid upon the table. And with that very general setup, I hope my colleagues will continue.

STEPHEN RADEMAKER: Let me add that it's a pleasure for me to be here as well. Thank you for inviting me.

I want to acknowledge at the outset of my remarks that concluding the START follow-on agreement is an important accomplishment for the Obama administration. If they ultimately succeed in persuading the Senate to ratify this treaty, they will have managed to accomplish something that no previous Democratic administration has accomplished. Not President

Kennedy, not President Johnson, not President Carter, not President Clinton, none of them managed to negotiate and bring into force a strategic arms control agreement between the United States and Russia. Now we have a lot of strategic arms control agreements between the United States and Russia, but all of them were negotiated and brought into force by Republican presidents. So this is a pretty significant thing for them to have been able to pull off, if they can get it through the Senate. I do have some concerns about the agreement which I want to touch on in my remarks.

First, at the conceptual level, there are two fundamental premises for this negotiation. Two reasons that the Obama administration made it a top priority. The first is, the "world-free-of-nuclear-weapons agenda", and there's already been a fair amount of discussion about that this morning. This is the idea that, if the United States provides leadership in the area of nuclear disarmament, that somehow this will provide us leverage in dealing with the real threats that we face in the area of nuclear nonproliferation, such as Iran and North Korea.

I agree with everything we've already heard this morning, that there really is no evidence to support this notion. It's in large measure wishful thinking, most vigorously advocated by groups that for a long time have had nuclear disarmament as their chief objective. And for them, this is essentially old wine in new bottles. It's a new and more convenient justification for policy prescriptions that they've been making for a long time.

The second conceptual underpinning for this negotiation was the reset with Russia. The effort by the new administration to radically change the nature of the US/Russian relationship, to make a clean break with the policies of the Bush administration and hopefully, in their view, create some goodwill between the United States and Russia that could be cashed-in, in other areas. For example, in increased Russian cooperation against Iran.

In that regard, I think, standing where we are today, you'd have to say, looking back over the past year, that this negotiation really didn't create a lot of goodwill between the United States and Russia. To the contrary, it fostered a great deal of suspicion and animosity between the two sides and that's where we are today. I don't know where we're going to be at the end of the ratification process, but there is a possibility that the suspicion and hard feelings will grow during the ratification process as the US Congress and the Russian Duma make demands and impose conditions on entry into force that accentuate some of the disagreements. But certainly, as of today, there isn't a whole lot of evidence that this negotiation has contributed to a new era of good feelings between the United States and Russia. Maybe that will change now that the negotiation is over and the two sides are cooperating on ratification, but that remains to be seen.

The fundamental purpose of the START follow-on agreement was to extend the verification regime that existed under the previous START treaty, and which expired on December 5th 2009. When the Obama administration came into office, extending that verification regime was seen as the low-hanging fruit in arms control. They thought this would be a quick negotiation that they could wrap up and then pave the way for more dramatic things they wanted to do in the area of arms control, such as persuading the Senate to reconsider its rejection of the Comprehensive Test Ban Treaty. And certainly they had the intention of then negotiating a second arms control agreement between the United States and Russia providing for much deeper reductions in nuclear force levels. The number that has been thrown about was that they wanted to negotiate a level below a thousand warheads on both sides, as compared to the fifteen fifty number that is in this treaty. Clearly they failed in the objective of wrapping up that negotiation by December 5th. And since December 5th of last year, we have lived in a world without strategic arms control verification. Which is certainly not an outcome that anybody, at least on the US side, wanted to see.

So clearly, negotiating this treaty proved harder than the Obama administration anticipated and it's fair for us today to ask, "what went wrong?" Why was this so hard? My analysis is that there were two basic surprises for the Obama administration once it entered into this negotiation. The first was a surprise to them. It was not a surprise to me and probably not a surprise to most of the people in this room. But the second one, frankly, was a surprise to me as well as the Obama administration.

The first surprise was that Russia did not reciprocate the Obama administration's enthusiasm for this negotiation. The Obama administration came to office quite excited about its agenda of a world free of nuclear weapons, and taking meaningful steps in that direction. It turns out Russia is a lot less enthusiastic about that. And the way it worked out, in fact, was that Russia chose to take advantage of the Obama administration's enthusiasm to try to drive very hard bargains on all the issues under negotiation.

Now as I say, this is not a surprise to me, but apparently it was a surprise to the Obama administration. It shouldn't be a surprise to most people. Arms control is fundamentally a process of negotiation. And we all, in our personal lives, have experience with negotiation. You know, when you go to buy a car, you don't walk into the dealership and say, I love this car. I'm not leaving here today without this car. How much would you sell it to me for? There's a technical term in the industry for people who negotiate like that. They're called suckers.

But looking back on the last year of negotiation between the United States and Russia, it's crystal clear that Russia thought they had a sucker on the line. And that explains why the December 5th deadline was not met. It explains why issues that should have been simple became very complicated. Based on the signals they were receiving, Russia believed they held the upper hand and so they tried to drive very hard bargains on all of these issues.

Now, in retrospect, you see the press reports where Obama administration officials point to a February conversation between President Obama and President Medvedev in which President Obama finally said to President Medvedev, "if you insist on these demands you're making, we're not going to have an agreement." And apparently that was the turning point. It was when the United States finally said to Russia, "you know, we can live without this agreement; we're not going to accept all of your demands." At that point, the Russians backed away and then, a month later, we get the announcement that they've come to an agreement. So that was obviously a productive conversation. I think we should commend the Obama administration for sending that signal—but maybe if they had had that conversation about a year earlier, we wouldn't have experienced the lapse in verification since December 5th that we're currently experiencing.

The second major surprise for me and the Obama administration in this negotiation was that Russia has lost a lot of its interest in verification. Now when I was in the Bush administration, Russia was very interested in verification. And they complained a lot that the Bush administration wasn't interested enough. They wanted verification for the Moscow treaty, and we didn't. We thought START verification was good enough. Once it turned out the US was interested in verification, Russia, I think, thought more clearly about its interests and decided it had much less interest in verification.

The verification regime that will accompany this treaty—we don't have the details of it yet—but it's clearly going to be much, much less robust than the verification that existed under the previous START agreement. Why is this? Well, a major reason, and perhaps the principal reason, is that Russia has come to see traditional arms control verification as a one-way street. For them, it is increasingly the case that in practice verification yields information to the United States and doesn't give corresponding information to Russia.

What do I mean by this? And why is this? Well, fundamentally, a lot of verification is directed at testing, development and production of systems. The United States isn't in that business anymore. Russia still is. So START verification, if continued in the future really is a one-way street, because Russia is continuing to test new missiles and continuing to produce new missiles and if they give us access, give us transparency into what they're doing, we can do the same, but since we're not doing anything, they're not getting any useful information. And so Russia has concluded they're really not interested in traditional transparency, because they are modernizing and the United States is not.

And I do think that this is a critically important point to bear in mind in the forthcoming debate in the Senate about ratification. Clearly one of the issues is going to be the call by Senate Republicans for increased US investment in the US nuclear weapons complex and in modernization of US nuclear delivery systems and warheads. And once that debate begins, I think you're going to hear a lot of voices saying, no, no, no, this is really dangerous. The United States shouldn't do this. It sends all the wrong signals. It's destabilizing.

Well, one of the lessons we've just learned from this negotiation is the exact opposite. That the failure of the United States to modernize is today jeopardizing our ability to continue negotiated verification measures between the United States and Russia. It is decreasing transparency, and in this world of strategic security and arms control, everybody agrees transparency is a really good thing. We're about to enter a world with a lot less transparency, all because Russia's is continuing to modernize and the United States isn't. Those are some of my introductory points.

This treaty has now been negotiated. It presumably soon will be before the Senate. What should the Senate do? I think it's premature, certainly for me, to make any recommendations. But I would point to some questions that I have and that I think the Senate needs to look at carefully in considering this treaty.

The first is the area of missile defense. We're told that there are no restrictions on missile defense in the treaty. That there's something in the preamble acknowledging a relationship between defense and offense, but beyond that, there will be no restrictions. But then we're also told that there will be a Russian unilateral statement upon signature about this issue.

We don't yet know what that unilateral statement will be. But I do think the Senate will have to look carefully at what the Russians say. It may be just a boilerplate statement that they will be watching US missile defense deployments carefully, and if they conclude that their nuclear deterrent has been threatened, they'll have to consider whether that's a threat to their supreme national interests, which would be a basis for a withdrawal from the treaty. If it is a self-evident assertion like that, maybe it won't be a problem.

On the other hand, they could be much more specific in their unilateral statement. For example, if they were to say in their unilateral statement that should the United States proceed with its declared policy of a phased adaptive deployment of missile defense capabilities in Europe, they will withdraw from the treaty, then, I think the Senate legitimately would have to ask whether there's really a meeting of the minds between the two parties. Is there actually an intention on both sides to live under this treaty, or are the Russians essentially coming to this wedding declaring that they want to get married, but they don't intend to live in holy matrimony? And, if that's the case, the Senate will need to consider whether there really is an agreement to approve.

My second area of concern is verification. As I've noted, verification is going to be much less robust than in the past. The Senate has to ask, "is it going to be sufficiently robust to provide assurance that Russia's not cheating on the key terms of the agreement?"

There are some areas that need to be looked at carefully. Telemetry, which in the past was required to be unencrypted, now is to be unencrypted for only five tests each year. And even that is to be negotiated on an annual basis, so really it's just an agreement to agree about what sort of telemetry to exchange.

I think there's a question there about missile defense, too. Will Russia seek to basically condition any telemetry exchange on US giving Russia telemetry on our missile defense tests? This is something that has never been done in the past. The Senate will have to look at this carefully as it considers this treaty.

Onsite inspections are clearly being scaled back from their baseline under START. How useful will the remaining inspections be?

Portal monitoring. This was the ability we had to permanently deploy inspectors outside the Russian production facilities for missiles. The inspectors would count the missiles as they were produced and left the factory. This will no longer continue. Again, the Russians' rationale was, "you're not producing missiles so we've got nothing to verify on your side. We're still producing missiles. We've got no interest in letting you verify what we're doing." How much of a concern is that for the United States' ability to monitor Russia's deployment of land-based mobile systems, which is the backbone of their nuclear capability these days?

A third area of concern is conventional strategic capabilities. How will prompt global strike and other conventional systems be affected by this treaty? It looks to me like we're allowed to have things like conventional Trident, but they would count against the ceilings of the treaty, which means this treaty does actually constrain conventional strategic capabilities that the US might deploy. Maybe I'm wrong about that. I haven't seen the text of the treaty, but that's the way it looks to me, based on what I know. I think the Senate needs to look at all these issues.

I also noted that a major area of discussion in the Senate will be US modernization of the nuclear force. Forty-one senators have already gone on record in that regard. So, that'll be an important part of the debate.

One final point, just looking forward to the future, I don't know what the fate of this treaty is in the Senate, but I am fairly confident in predicting that we're not going to see another strategic arms control negotiation between the United States and Russia. I think this last one has left a bitter taste in the mouth of both sides. So, I think that doing another one of these isn't actually going to contribute to resetting relations between the US and Russia. It might actually have the opposite effect.

And second, if there were a follow-on negotiation, the issues to be dealt with would be much more complex than in this treaty. Because on the US side, as Kurt Volker pointed out in his comments, I don't think we can negotiate further nuclear reductions at the strategic level without also beginning to negotiate some sort of restrictions on non-strategic nuclear deployments.

In the past, the idea was there were so many strategic warheads deployed, that we could ignore the whole universe of tactical nuclear warheads, that they were basically irrelevant. But as you reduce the number of strategic weapons, you eventually come to have fewer strategic warheads than tactical nuclear warheads, and I think it becomes impossible to tell yourself the tactical warheads still don't matter.

And so I think in the next negotiation it will be essential to address tactical warheads. And based on everything I know, this is a complete nonstarter with Russia. Russia has no intention of negotiating on non-strategic nuclear warheads for one very simple reason—and I've had Russian government officials tell me this without any hint of irony or embarrassment—they consider themselves to be more dependent on their tactical nuclear warheads today than ever before. And they simply have no intention of reducing their reliance on them.

So the next negotiation, if there were to be one, would have to address that issue from our side. I don't think there's any interest in Russia doing that. From the Russian perspective, I think it's crystal clear from this last negotiation that any follow-on negotiation would have to deal with missile defense from their point of view, and on the US side, that's a nonstarter.

So for all those reasons, while this may be the first strategic arms control agreement brought into force by a Democratic administration, I think it will be the last one brought into force by the Obama administration.

TOM SCHEBER: I want to get into the details of the force nuclear structure itself and, in particular, I want to try to take your minds away from the number 1550—the warhead ceiling in the New START Treaty. People can try to tell you that any particular number of warheads should be sufficient, but more important are the details behind the number. So, setting aside 1550, let's look at the details from what we currently understand about the combined effects from the new treaty and what we know so far about the Nuclear Posture Review. How well does that posture enable the United States to be able to respond to events in the future?

The bipartisan Strategic Posture Commission reported out about a year ago. That commission said that there were two increasingly important attributes of the US force posture: flexibility and resilience. Now, we could think about flexibility in simplistic terms as providing the president a range of tools to deal with a crisis. First, we should consider flexibility in the near term. What will the treaty and the NPR together leave us? And what might the president want to do? The president could want to signal intent by changing the alert level of forces. He may—in extreme conditions—call for a strike to protect our allies or United States forces. US forces may need to be used rapidly or we may need to be able to adjust the posture while we wait. Our weapons may need to have very special characteristics to penetrate enemy defenses and to produce particular kinds of effects.

So what does the treaty and the NPR leave us in the near future? The Nuclear Posture Review, being released today, calls for the retention of a nuclear triad, as we have now. Little damage is done there. Currently, we have about 835 delivery vehicles if we count ballistic missiles that are active and not in overhaul, as well as heavy bombers. To comply with the new treaty the United States will have to reduce about 130 to 140 delivery systems, ballistic missiles or bombers. These are fairly modern systems, that each have a decade or more of life remaining. Will the administration also change the posture of those forces? That remains to be seen. It does not appear to be a primary focus of the NPR.

Of most concern is the issue reported in the *Washington Post* today, the issue of declaratory policy. It reported that the administration will change the long-standing negative security assurances which were intended to cause adversaries uncertainty over what actions would compel the US to respond with nuclear weapons. The current policy of "ambiguity" has been considered an important element of deterrence. The more restrictive negative security assurance policy that will be put forward by the Obama administration gives states with chemical weapons and biological weapons—states that are also parties to the NPT and in good standing—almost a guarantee that we will not use nuclear weapons. We'll have to look at the exact wording as it comes out. But early indications report that the new policy statement would call for an overwhelming response with conventional weapons in response to use of chemical and biological weapons. Probably not a good thing to do; deterrence is in the mind of the adversary and who knows what's in the mind of leaders like Kim Jong-Il in North Korea and Ahmadinejad in Iran? Do they understand the nuanced messages that we intend? How will they perceive U.S. statements of restraint?

So far, for the near term, I'd give the Obama administration fairly passing grades. They will retain a mix of strategic nuclear forces. They retain one of the two non-strategic nuclear forces. They will commit to modernize the dual-capable aircraft or at least to have plans to modernize the next generation of dual-capable aircraft for NATO. It is likely that they will announce the retirement of TLAM/N, the sea-launched cruise missile which hasn't been deployed since 1991. So the near-term force posture will not change dramatically and will probably provide a flexible set of tools—response options for the president—for the near term.

Of concern is the longer term. I want to discuss a term that the Strategic Posture Commission called "resilience." How do we posture ourselves so that we can be able to respond in case the world turns out to be a much more hostile, much nastier place? Do we have a plan B? And what might cause the need for a plan B? There are a variety of reasons. A nuclear-armed adversary or a WMD-armed adversary could significantly increase the size or the capability of its arsenal. Several nuclear-armed adversaries could form an alliance against the United States. What comes to mind is a China-Russia alliance against the United States. We could also experience a technical failure—a failure in a leg of our strategic forces. These forces are aging; most were designed in the 70s and 80s. We could also experience a failure in part of our critical infrastructure for nuclear force sustainment. The infrastructure which has been fairly fragile and limping along in recent years supports the nuclear force. If a failure caused the infrastructure to be shut down for a period of time, delaying warhead repairs or life extension programs, adjustments in warheads loaded on different legs of the force may be needed. Finally, policy changes in the future could require changes in the characteristics of the forces or the balance among the legs of the nuclear triad.

Resilience in the strategic posture is important and should be retained. It has been a key component of all previous Nuclear Posture Reviews. The Clinton administration in the first Nuclear Posture Review (NPR) in 1994 unveiled its "lead but hedge" strategy in which we would draw down from START levels to START-II, but retain the ability and extra warheads to redeploy back to the START level. The Bush administration, in 2001, had something similar to the "lead but hedge" strategy. They gave it a different term called "responsive capability." Essentially, it looked a lot the same. But in reality it differed in the view that non-deployed warheads in storage did not provide a long-term, viable approach for resilience. What was needed was to fix the infrastructure to be able to repair, modify, or build new warheads when needed—they wouldn't last forever. The 2001 NPR called for an improved ability to build new warheads, if needed, but to retain force structure—the submarines, the ICBMs and the bombers. Last year, the bipartisan Commission on the Strategic Posture endorsed a continuing hedge strategy because of the uncertainties ahead.

What do you need for a hedge strategy? What initiatives that would support a hedge should we look for in the Obama administration's NPR? A hedge strategy needs three components. First, a force structure. The force structure provides additional capacity which can be used to adjust the relative balance of deployed warheads in the force or, if needed, to deploy more than 1550 strategic warheads. The initial plan to deploy 1550 warheads may need to be periodically adjusted for deterrence of adversaries and assurance of allies. We also need some combination of a stockpile of non-deployed warheads and an infrastructure that is ready and capable to fix warheads and forces when they experience reliability problems. This infrastructure must also be ready to build the next generation of strategic forces when the existing forces reach the end of service life.

The new treaty requires that we eliminate about 130 to 140 delivery vehicles. So the excess capacity will be decreased. The president has reported and last month announced that he would reduce the stockpile, so we expect the stockpile to be reduced. For the infrastructure, there is good news. I think there's about seven hundred million dollars additional for the NNSA, the National Nuclear Security Agency, which funds the nuclear weapon laboratories and the plants. They have been long neglected. This will help get the labs and the plants to where they can conduct the surveillance, the modernization, the life extension of the warheads that are needed. It's not clear yet if the NPR will have the same type of funding to sustain DoD critical technologies. We have some critical technologies that you may have seen referred to by DoD Under Secretary Ash Carter in his remarks about rare technologies—technologies that are not regularly exercised and in danger of going away. Clearly, large-diameter, solid rocket boosters is a technology that we should worry about. The one plant remaining is largely inactive. Other niche technologies also exist, such as nuclear hardening, for which we will have to make a dedicated effort to sustain. Without a dedicated sustainment effort, those technologies will be lost.

Early reports of the Nuclear Posture Review claim that there will be a commitment to do nothing new associated with nuclear warheads. I challenge you, when you go back to your offices, do a search in your favorite online dictionary and look at all the definitions of "new" and as it may relate to anything new for nuclear forces; in other words, no new capabilities. "New" can be used to mean: different, newly-produced, etc. Reportedly, the commitment in the NPR will be to "no new designs." This is essentially committing to the life extension or replacement of Cold War-era designed forces and warheads. Those may not be the best and most effective capabilities to deter future adversaries or in which our allies are most assured. The director of Lawrence Livermore recently sent a letter to Representative Turner, in which he talked about limitations of life extension programs for warheads. The current approach to life extension programs for warheads—what we're doing now—is to just replace components as they wear out. It's similar to the way you keep a car running after it gets old. The life extension program approach exercises only a limited portion of the infrastructure intellectual base—that required to make life extension repairs. It does not fully exercise the overall intellectual base required to maintain the nuclear force for the long term. He concluded that it will become increasingly difficult to preserve the base of human capital if their skills are not exercised routinely.

Lastly, let me look to the future and add a couple of remarks to what Steve Rademaker has said about the next treaty. We see that the Obama administration is already talking about the next treaty. The strategic posture commission indicated that, most important, would be to negotiate a treaty to reduce non-strategic nuclear weapons. The commission cautioned the new administration to keep START replacement simple. This administration, however, has made adversarial Cold War style nuclear arms control, once again, the centerpiece of the US-Russia relationship. The resulting New START treaty allows Russia to continue its planned, extensive nuclear modernization without any concessions. If you read the Russian press, they talk about their plans and already being well below the 700 strategic delivery vehicles allowed under the new treaty. The new treaty drags the US down to a similar level when we had not planned or been required to do so. Of concern, the Russian forces will be more heavily MIRVed than we've seen in the recent past. Previously, both U.S. and Russians arms control negotiators agreed that that we would seek to move away from heavily MIRVed forces and that fewer warheads on ballistic missiles was "stabilizing" for both sides. In general, in my judgment, in this new treaty the U.S. has largely given away any remaining leverage to negotiate with Russia on issues of greater importance, such as the imbalance of tactical nuclear weapons.

In conclusion, on the three issues that I touched on: Do the administration's nuclear policies leave us flexibility in the near-term? Here they get pretty good, at least passing grades. Second, does it support "resilience" and prepare us for the future? That's where there is the significant concern. Finally, does it retain leverage for future negotiations? I would give the administration a failing grade in this third area.

BAKER SPRING: Thank you very much. We've got a small amount of time for questions. If you could identify yourself. And keep yourself to a simple straightforward question so we can get in as many as possible in this limited time.

QUESTIONER: Thank you, gentlemen, for your remarks. Tom and Tom and Stephen. I would like to ask the same question. The argument has been that the failures to reign in both Iran and North Korea was because the Bush administration was not committed to either counter-proliferation, but particularly, relationship between proliferation and terrorism. I say that, cause I have now a thousand e-mail exchanges, one of the top arms controllers in this country, that we've been doing over the last five weeks, which I'm preserving for, with his permission, publication. That's been his major theme. We had to do all these things in order to change the tone and the atmospherics and that then will get the international community together to go after Iran and North Korea. I'd like your comment.

TOM DONNELLY: Without knowing who your interlocutor is here, I'm sure I would recognize the name if he were here, I mean, it just seems like he's looking through the wrong end of the telescope to me. Iran and North Korea, in fact, right, everybody, we're the only people who think that, that the future utility of nuclear weapons is diminishing. The entire rest of the planet, be they, you know, aspiring nuclear states or small arsenal nuclear states like Iran and North Korea—or even, you know, medium and large sized nuclear powers—clearly believe that nuclear weapons, you know, have a continued strategic value and that's why they want to retain them. That's why people who don't have them want to get them and so, you know, I see a greater international appetite for both retaining and acquiring or even expanding nuclear capabilities by basically everybody but us.

So, you know, in order to understand or to try to understand what the North Koreans and the Iranians think about nuclear weapons and the way that other people think about nuclear weapons, they have to think about what their strategic perspective among the world is and, you know, just look at the behavior of these people. It's quite different than ours and our ability to induce them. It's difficult enough to coerce them, but to employ soft power and persuasion to get them to renounce capabilities that they value very highly is a very difficult task. And so far, the track record's pretty unimpressive.

STEPHEN RADEMAKER: I'm quite familiar with the notion that if the US provides leadership in reducing our nuclear force levels and demonstrates real commitment to abolishing our nuclear arsenal, that will somehow help solve the Iran and North Korea problems. How? Well, one idea would be that Iran and North Korea would be so inspired by our example that they would decide to abandon their nuclear ambitions. They would say, "I don't know what we were thinking, but we've changed our mind. We're just not interested in these weapons anymore, because America has shown us the right way." That is so ludicrous on its face that I don't think anybody really argues that anymore. I think early on there were some people who made that argument, but it's just laughable.

So then how will this concept work? Well, you have to fall back to what I think you were suggesting in your question, which is that our ability to achieve a global diplomatic consensus against Iran and North Korea will be enhanced, and that somehow diplomacy, which hasn't worked up until now, will suddenly start working. Because of what I don't know—affection for the United States, inspiration by our leadership, renewed commitment by all the nations of the world to preventing any further nuclear proliferation.

The premise of this line of thought is that there are a bunch of countries out there that would do more, could do more, but aren't doing more against Iran and North Korea, because they're really disappointed in what we're doing. And so those countries are sitting there, waiting. And if we do the right thing, then they'll change policy and instead of not cooperating as they have in the past, they'll start cooperating.

No one has ever been able to identify to me who these countries are and what it is that they would be prepared to do in the future that they're refusing to do today. I used to work in this world full time when I was at the State Department and there are a lot of countries out there that are really passionate about nuclear disarmament and nuclear proliferation. Sweden, you know, they really feel this deeply. New Zealand, they're passionate about this. But are you really telling me that there are things that Sweden could do today to contribute to a solution to the Iran nuclear proliferation problem that they're not doing? Because they're really mad, they're really disappointed about US policy? Again, to me that's just laughable. It's demonstrably untrue. So I think you sort of have to take the earnest Western antinuclear countries out of the equation.

What's left? You've got Egypt, you've got South Africa, Indonesia. Call them the nonaligned countries with a grievance. But what's their grievance?

I spent a lot of time dealing with Egypt at the last NPT review conference. They've got a big grievance. But it's with Israel. It has nothing to do with the United States. We could give up every last nuclear weapon the United States has. Egypt would not be satisfied. Their agenda is about Israel. And until Israel does a whole series of things they're demanding,

Egypt's not going to be satisfied. Recall at the last NPT review conference, it was Egypt single-handedly that tied the conference in knots. And the reason they tied it in knots was about their concerns related to Israel. South Africa, just using them as an example—is South Africa actually prepared to do more against Iran? And even if they were, what could they do?

We know what the obstacle today is to sanctions and meaningful diplomatic pressure on Iran. The obstacle is Russia and China. They're holding up action at the UN security council. They are nuclear weapons states. They are not invested in the world without nuclear weapons agenda. Whatever their reasons are for standing in the way of UN sanctions on Iran, it has nothing to do with their disappointment at the failure of the United States to more rapidly move forward with implementation of article six of the NPT. Because if they were so committed to that, they would be giving up their own nuclear weapons.

So, the real problem today is with countries that are nuclear weapon states that have other diplomatic priorities that for them outweigh the importance of dealing with Iran and North Korea. So, this has become an article of faith, and unfortunately some pretty serious people like Henry Kissinger and George Schultz have signed on to it. I've never had a chance to talk to Henry Kissinger about this, but I'd like to. It just does not withstand analysis. When you sit down and look at it, take it case by case, country by country, issue by issue, what you could do, what you'd expect other countries to do against Iran, it does not add up. This is a fiction that is, as I said in my remarks, propagated primarily by groups that have always wanted nuclear disarmament and they've come up with this as a really convenient vehicle for putting forward arguments that they've been making for decades.

QUESTIONER: I'm Susan Cornwell with Reuters and forgive me, I had to step out for a minute, so I may have missed something, but I just wondered, even with all the concerns that you raise about the START treaty, whether it's really possible that the Senate would reject it. You know, the administration has said, you know, all these treaties in the end, they're confirmed. 95 to 3 or, you know, 98 to 2. And I'm just wondering if anybody thinks this treaty is really far enough out of the mainstream, you know, or the past examples that it's actually in danger of being rejected. And especially on the verification thing. I mean, you made the point that the verification's not as good as it was, but won't you get senators saying, "well, it may not be as good as it was, but it looks like the best we're going to get." It's, perhaps because of the things that you, Mr. Rademaker, said about, you know, the difficulties of going back and negotiating with the Russians, it would seem unlikely that, you know, they could take it back and say, oh well, let's negotiate some tougher verification measures. So isn't it likely that they'll go ahead and approve this? Is anyone there willing to predict that they won't? Thank you.

STEPHEN RADEMAKER: I think you make some valid points, particularly on verification. It's disappointing what's in this treaty, what we know of what's in the treaty. But certainly the argument will be made that it's better than what we have today, which since December 5th has been nothing. So some transparency, some verification is better than no verification. Absolutely. That argument will be made and I think it will resonate with a lot of senators.

I do think on the missile defense issue, we need to see, as I say, is there actually a meeting of the minds between Russia and the United States, or is Russia going to tell us on Thursday that they only intend to abide by this treaty if the United States backs away from commitments that President Obama himself has made with respect to the deployment of missile defenses? And if that's actually the Russian position, then I think some senators will ask, "what sort of agreement is this and is there an agreement here for us to approve?" But on balance, I think you're basically correct.

I would predict that the single biggest issue in the Senate's consideration of this treaty will be the question of modernization of US nuclear forces, and the Obama administration recognizes this. They're already proposing increased funding in that area. Pardon my cynicism, but I don't think they're doing this because they are ideologically committed to modernization of the US nuclear force. I think this was a political calculation that they came to some months ago, that they needed to do this in order to lay the groundwork for approval of this treaty. And I think they still have hope that maybe one day they can get the CTBT approved, and they would need to do the same thing there to mollify the critics.

But I would just simply predict that the way this debate will unfold in this area is that on the Republican side, you'll hear a lot of members saying the Administration's proposed increases are not adequate, and there have to be even bigger increases in funding, and more concrete commitments by the administration about what it's prepared to do in this area. I don't know how that will unfold, but one could imagine that taking some time for the respective positions to materialize and the negotiations to take place and an agreement to be reached. It's difficult without seeing the text of the treaty to say there are no fatal problems. I did not predict in my remarks that it would be defeated. I just outlined some areas that I thought would be of concern to the Senate and would come under a great deal of scrutiny.

TOM SCHEBER: On Thursday (the day the New START Treaty is to be signed) there will be a lot of questions unanswered. It's been stated that the treaty itself—the basic treaty text, and the protocols—will be ready. However, the technical annexes that explain in detail how each process will be conducted will not be completed at that time. The first rule of arms control is typically that nothing is agreed until everything is agreed. So the president will sign a treaty that is two-thirds finished on Thursday. I think a lot of senators will be asking their staffs to dig into the details, to check the carefully worded statements that the administration has put forward, and to examine carefully those statements to understand the meanings that both sides have taken away from the negotiations. Because it's a very detailed treaty, perhaps more detailed than it needed to be, this process will take some time to understand and determine whether or not serious problem exist with the treaty.

TOM DONNELLY: Real quickly. I don't want to predict, but I would like to offer sort of a narrative. So if things go wrong, here's how they might go wrong. I think Steve was quite right; if they do go wrong, it's because the debate becomes broader rather than just a narrow debate about the provisions of the treaty. Steve mentioned modernization and his final comment was about that test ban treaty, I think to the degree that creeps into the debate, that's probably bad for getting, you know, two-thirds of the Senate to sign up to it. I would also say that Secretary Gates's role in this is really going to be quite critical, just to read one quote from last October. He said, to be blunt, "There's absolutely no way we can maintain a credible deterrent and reduce the number of weapons in our stockpile without resorting to testing our stockpile or pursuing a modernization program." So how does Secretary Gates, you know, square the circle that appears to be being drawn by the White House? If he's credible at it, then they'll probably do pretty well. If he's less credible at it, then, again, you could be through.

BAKER SPRING: Let me just make one point, too, which is that if you look at the treaty exclusively, you may not be seeing all of the problems. The question is, what are the external linkages to the treaty? The obvious one, of course, is in missile defense. One of the things that we in the public will likely never see, almost certainly will never see is something I assume the Senate would have a very keen interest in, which is the negotiating record of the treaty. What exactly were the back and forth between the US negotiators and the Russian negotiators with regard to what could be described as unofficial deals? And I think that that's the kind of thing that could run off the rails for the president very quickly. ▪

The Dangers of Nuclear Disarmament

A PANEL DISCUSSION WITH THE
NEW DETERRENT WORKING GROUP

FRANK GAFFNEY: My name is Frank Gaffney. I am the president of the Center for Security Policy, and I'm delighted to be hosting this presentation by members of an informal group we call the New Deterrent Working Group.

Members of the Working Group include some of the most distinguished and thoughtful practitioners of nuclear deterrence I have had the privilege of knowing and working with over the past thirty some years. They are men and women who have had personal experience both with the policy and the programmatic aspects of the issues at the top of our agenda today

This discussion included: **Frank J. Gaffney, Jr.**, President, the Center for Security Policy; **Rep. Mike Turner** (R-Ohio), Ranking Member of the Strategic Forces Subcommittee of the House Armed Services Committee; **Paula DeSutter**, former Assistant Secretary of State for Verification and Compliance; **Vice Adm. Robert Monroe**, US Navy (Ret.), former Director, the Defense Nuclear Agency; **Adm. James "Ace" Lyons**, US Navy (Ret.), former Commander-in-Chief, US Pacific Fleet; and **Peter Huessy**, President, GeoStategic Analysis, Inc.

as the president completes the new START treaty, with its signing in Prague. In addition, there is the Nuclear Posture Review released on Tuesday, the Nuclear Security Summit next week, the Nuclear Non-Proliferation Treaty review conference next month and the Comprehensive Test Ban Treaty ratification debate looming at some point down the road. So, all of these items are very much on the minds of the members of the New Deterrent Working Group.

You have at your places a monograph the Group published last year that is a helpful introduction to many of these issues. Entitled *Nuclear Deterrence in the 21ˢᵗ Century: Getting It Right,* this booklet includes important ideas, information and quotes from some of our most distinguished senior civilian and military leaders with regard to the nuclear deterrent and what it takes to preserve it. We hope that it will be a further resource to you in enriching your understanding of these issues.

Above and beyond what you'll be hearing from this distinguished panel about today, we are going to invite **Congressman Mike Turner**, who is joining us by phone, to say a few words. Rep. Turner, of course, is the ranking Republican on the Strategic Forces Subcommittee of the House Armed Services Committee. He is one of the most knowledgeable, certainly one of the most thoughtful and indisputably one of the most directly engaged legislators on either side of Capitol Hill on the issues that we will be talking about today.

I know you are taking some time from your family to be with us, Congressman Turner, and I'm very grateful to you for what you do when you are performing your day job and even more so for spending some time with us when you are supposed to be having some time off.

REP. MIKE TURNER: I want to thank all of you for your thoughtful approach to what are important issues on our national security. The issue of the Nuclear Posture Review (NPR) that we have before us, and of course START, it bears the level of scrutiny that I know you all are going to give to it as we look to how can we best protect this country.

I have some concerns about the president's announcement on the limitations that are going to be stated in the NPR. It's a unilateral action on behalf of the president. Part of the concern that I have is that the president has made this broad statement of a world without nuclear weapons, wanting to go to zero, instead of it being just a human values statement, a broader statement for us all to embrace as a goal of humanity. He is too far down the road on his own.

We have to be concerned, because each step along the way where there's a change in our nuclear policy is a signal for what the next step will be.

This approach raises serious concerns. This is a case of the administration prospectively indicating how it believes others will respond, in the future, without any historical basis. We've not seen that—as the United States has decreased its arsenal and Russia has decreased its arsenal, we've not seen an abandonment by foreign nations to seek nuclear weapons or nuclear capabilities. So, there's really not a historical basis for the president saying that this type of change, that we would undertake, will result in a safer world for us.

The other issue, obviously, is what does it mean? I think the president doesn't necessarily mean that he would not defend the United States with every available system we have to the extent that it would be necessary. And to that extent, I think the foreign audience will find that the NPR statement is meaningless. So I do have some concerns as to how this is implemented and what it really does say—I do have some belief that it's not necessarily good for achieving the objectives that the president has as his goal.

FRANK GAFFNEY: Thank you very much, congressman. The Nuclear Posture Review is, of course, the focus of yesterday's attention. Did you have any thoughts that you would like to share with us before we let you go on the strategic arms treaty signed today?

REP. MIKE TURNER: Yes, I think that the missile defense aspect of it is something that we should be concerned about. The Russians are signaling that they believe that the language can be used to limit the expansion of the United States in missile defense. The president is saying, of course, that it's not going to be something that will limit our pursuit of missile defense. That's an area where there appears to be a conflict. And one where the Russians are already signaling and reserving the right to withdraw if missile defense is vigorously pursued. I think that's an area that we have to be concerned about and also we don't really have the details from the administration as to how the agreement will be implemented. What will be the mixture? How will it affect the Triad? What will be left?

FRANK GAFFNEY: Thank you, sir. We look forward to sharing with you the fruits of this conversation. And again, thank you so much for taking some time with us from family time.

REP. MIKE TURNER: Sure. Thank you.

FRANK GAFFNEY: Let me now introduce, in turn, the folks on our panel. I'm going to say a few words and then turn it over to **Vice Admiral Robert Monroe** USN (Retired). Among many other distinguished positions Adm. Monroe held in the Navy and in the Defense Department, he is the former Director of the Defense Nuclear Agency—an agency that is no more, sadly. DNA's disestablishment is, I am afraid, a reflection of a lack of seriousness about the nuclear enterprise that has taken hold in the years since Bob left government service. Admiral Monroe is an expert on the underpinnings of the nuclear deterrent: industrial, technological, scientific. And we will hear from him shortly about the sort of context in which our conversations are taking place today.

We will then go to **Peter Huessy**, who is the president of GeoStrategic Analysis. He's better known here in Washington as the man who runs a highly influential breakfast series for the National Defense University Foundation. These are really among the most serious venues in Washington for discourse with those responsible for the strategies, the programs, the policies affecting nuclear deterrence, missile defense and related issues. And they're starting next week. A plug here for those breakfasts, if you haven't gotten on the invitee list, contact Peter.

We'll then hear from the Honorable **Paula DeSutter**, who most recently served as the Assistant Secretary of State for the Bureau of Verification, Compliance and Implementation. A vital role in the past. It quite possibly will be an increasingly important one as we hear about some of the difficulties with verifying things like the New START treaty, the Comprehensive Test Ban Treaty, and other issues if you care to get into them, for example, space arms control and the like.

Our cleanup batter will be **Admiral James "Ace" Lyons**, US Navy (Retired). Adm. Lyons formerly served as the Commander-in-Chief, US

Pacific Fleet. And Ace will be providing the perspective of a man with operational responsibilities in the United States military for our nuclear deterrence about the need to ensure that it is credible—and the potential implications for it no longer being seen as such.

Let me just say a couple of words by way of introduction to the topic. I had the privilege of serving President Reagan in the Defense Department a long time ago in a position that was then known as the Deputy Assistant Secretary of Defense for Nuclear Forces and Arms Control Policy. I had some experience prior to that on the Senate Armed Services Committee, staffing the committee on the Strategic Forces Subcommittee and then finished up my time at the Pentagon acting as the Assistant Secretary of Defense with the responsibility for the US/Soviet policy portfolio.

So the nuclear enterprise is not only an avocation for me. And it troubles me, professionally and personally, that what I consider to be the most momentous national security decisions in memory are being taken with so little public awareness, let alone informed debate. And the consequences of taking such momentous steps without appropriate deliberation could be nothing short of catastrophic. I use such strong terms advisedly.

We are, for the first time in our history, led by a Commander-in-Chief who not only believes in a rhetorical sense that it would be desirable to live in a world without nuclear weapons, but who believes he can bring it about. To be sure, he has, of late, taken to clarifying that that may not happen right away. It may not happen, he said today, in his lifetime. Indeed, it will not.

Mr. Obama nonetheless is changing American nuclear weapons policy and deterrent strategy and programs in ways that he explicitly says are designed to advance that goal. I believe the problem that arises from such a course of action is that the president is aggressively disarming the one nation in the world that he can disarm. That happens to be ours.

Worse yet, President Obama is doing so at a moment when no other nuclear weapon state, or for that matter any obvious nuclear wannabe state, has evinced the slightest evidence that they are going to follow his lead. To the contrary, every nuclear weapons state is modernizing its nuclear arsenal. The most dangerous of these have hot production lines to do so, something we do not. They have a skilled work force dedicated to supporting that activity, something we increasingly do not.

My colleagues will elaborate on all of these points with far greater expertise than I, but let me simply conclude by saying the world will not be a safer place if the United States is perceived as having weakened, let alone mortally damaged its nuclear deterrent posture. And for reasons that we'll be discussing with you today, I believe that is what is afoot.

We welcome the chance to discuss this with you—and, hopefully through the miracle of the television and the internet media as well as through the good offices of those of you here, to engage many others, as well—in order to inform and catalyze the kind of debate that these momentous national security decisions demand, especially in this kind of dangerous world.

So with that, let me welcome Vice Admiral Robert Monroe to pick up the baton and run with it.

ROBERT MONROE: Thank you, Frank. I'm glad to be here this morning, and I thank you for coming.

I believe this Administration's nuclear weapons policy and programs are seriously misguided and dangerously ill-advised. Those of us who hold these views must speak out, so mistakes can be corrected.

I'll limit my comments here today to four topics: First, a world without nuclear weapons is neither achievable nor desirable. Second, "devaluing" nuclear weapons is exactly the wrong way to go. Third, proliferation, the #1 nuclear weapons threat facing the world, must be stopped. Fourth, deterrence is vital—but totally misunderstood.

President Obama has made a "world without nuclear weapons" a preeminent national goal. But no one can describe how to get there. And no one knows how to remain there when nuclear weapons technology is widely understood, and fissile material will progressively become more available. And no one can even imagine how to verify the absence of nuclear weapons in other states and organizations.

Now it's highly inadvisable to establish a national goal without knowing how to meet it; but it's even worse to launch rapid, far-reaching, unilateral disarmament actions to initiate movement. Many actions being taken today are contrary to America's real national security needs.

As far as the undesirability of total nuclear disarmament, without strong responsible nuclear weapons states to maintain order, we would exist in a world of frequent nuclear detonations by aggressors, rogue states, failed and failing states, fanatics, proxy organizations, terrorists, extortionists, criminals, even disaffected individuals.

Moving to my second topic, one of President Obama's principal initiatives is to devalue nuclear weapons. This also is highly counterproductive.

Nuclear weapons have repeatedly demonstrated their immense value to the world. They brought an end to the most destructive war in history, in the process saving a million lives. For a half century thereafter they prevented a much more devastating war. Also during that Cold War, nuclear weapons were a huge factor in preventing proliferation. Even today, the presence of nuclear weapons in some hands is acting as a damper on their use by others. Furthermore, by their very presence, nuclear weapons have banished large scale conventional conflicts that killed tens of millions in the past. And for generations to come, nuclear weapons in the hands of responsible states are the only hope for the world. Nuclear weapons should be awarded the Nobel Peace Prize.

On a practical level, nuclear weapons require the very best people America can produce as laboratory scientists, design engineers, military specialists and operators. If nuclear weapons are vilified, which is in process, these exceptional people won't choose these careers. And the results will be catastrophic. And what of deterrence? For deterrence to be effective, our adversary must be absolutely convinced of both our capability and our will to use military force. Devaluation destroys our image of firmness and strength.

Now let's consider proliferation, the most serious threat facing the world. For twenty years we've watched two rogue states, Iran and North Korea, develop nuclear weapons production capability, and we've not had the gumption to stop them. If these two states succeed—and they're very near it—their neighbors in the Mideast and Asia will go nuclear in response. This will trigger a global cascade of proliferation. The resulting worldwide availability of nuclear weapons and fissile material will lead to a world of nuclear horror and chaos, from which there is no return.

Future historians will ask—about us: how could they let this happen? What were they thinking? Our course of action is clear. Nonproliferation requires enforcement! There must be a cop on the beat. And as the world stands today, this responsibility falls on the United States. We must stop Iran and North Korea, by military force if necessary.

The Nonproliferation Treaty itself shows the way. The treaty creates two tiers of states: five nuclear weapons states, and the remainder (now 184 states) without nuclear weapons. We're now caving in to international pressure for nuclear disarmament, when we should be emphasizing the implicit responsibility of these five—collegially if possible, separately if necessary—to police the treaty and prevent proliferation.

Lastly, let's move to deterrence. Never have so many national leaders used a word so frequently without understanding it. Deterrence is all about fear. In fact, that's the root of the word. We create the fear by making a threat. For example, in the case of Iran, we threaten them as follows: "If you do not dismantle your nuclear weapons facilities, we will do it, with military force." Always use the term "military force." Never mention nuclear weapons, but never exclude them.

We then convince Iranian leaders by a continuing series of major reinforcing actions that we're prepared to do exactly what we say. We accelerate conventional weapons procurement, we visibly test weapons, destroying mirror-image targets. We intensify training, conduct major exercises, raise global alert levels, deploy forces to the adversary's area. On the nuclear side we resume underground nuclear testing and commence developing new-design nuclear weapons tailored to today's threats. To reinforce our threat, we place the nation on a wartime footing. This is deterrence, and it really works. The payoff is it alters our adversary's behavior. He complies with our aims *without* violence.

Deterrence isn't something you *have*, like nuclear weapons in storage sites. It's something you *do*. Hundreds of major national actions must be taken to convince the adversary that you're preparing to strike unless he complies with your threat. And deterrence must be focused on a single adversary. A deterrence strategy that works with state "A" isn't going to work against state "B."

In summary, it's 1938 for us. Our Chamberlain is so desirous of "peace in our time", that he doesn't remember the seven years of war and sixty million dead that 1938's wishful thinking cost the world. Thank you.

FRANK GAFFNEY: Bob, thank you very much. A sober, and I think timely, analysis. Peter Huessy on the strategic arms reduction treaty, the NPR, missile defense and related subjects.

PETER HUESSY: Thank you, Frank. It's an honor to be here. Thank you very much. It's an honor to be here. This is Peter Huessy, President of Geostrategic Analysis. I'm going to go through a number of issues.

But let me start with the commonalities of the NPR in 2002 by President Bush, the 1994 by President Clinton, and the 2010 by President Obama. They all talked about reducing proliferation. The emphasis, particularly after 9/11, became reducing proliferation to not only terrorist groups, but terror masters as Mike Ledeen calls them, particularly Iran and North Korea. There was an emphasis on reducing instability, meaning in a crisis, no one's going to grab for the nuclear pistol. The third commonality was to reduce nuclear warheads consistent with stability and consistent with deterrent needs. Expand on Nunn-Lugar and the Defense Threat Reduction Act and clean up loose nukes and loose nuclear material, both in the civilian sector and in the military sector. Preserve a nuclear triad. All three NPRs do that. And we are not going to rule out going first, and we are not going to de-alert our weapons.

Although the three NPRs had different emphases, they all have those common themes. What is new? In 2001, we had no deployed missile defenses. Zero in the United States. By the end of President Bush's term, we are now approaching over a thousand deployed or planned deployed interceptors. President Obama, contrary to what I would have expected, added two hundred THAAD and Aegis standard missile interceptors to that number to be procured over the next few years. Unfortunately, he cut back our national missile defense in Alaska and California and canceled the Polish interceptor site and the Czech radar which were to defend Europe and the United States from long-range Iranian rockets.

On the other hand, as Ash Carter and others have said, missile defense is now front and center of American security policy. That is a common theme in the last two NPRs. But it was not a major theme in the first NPR. This administration has said over four years they want to lock down nuclear material. God bless them. I hope they can get there. It is an extraordinarily ambitious agenda. We had under Bush, after an initial review, record amounts requested for the DTRA and Nunn-Lugar. It was approved by Congress. That was increased again in 2007 and '8, and then again in this last budget of the President. One of the programs begun under President Bush was something that my friend Madeleine Creighton calls "megatons to megawatts"—taking Russian nuclear material and putting it in nuclear power plants and burning it, so you really have taken nuclear weapons fuel and eliminated it. So I would caution people to say that this NPR is somehow so totally new and so totally different any more than the 2002 NPR was a radical change from 1994. There have been changes. The world has changed.

The second issue is compliance, which Paula will talk about, but my concern is, how do you determine that a country is compliant with a non-proliferation treaty so that if they use biological weapons against us, we're not going to respond with nuclear weapons? As Keith Payne wrote today in the *Washington Times*, in an e-mail that Bill Gertz pointed out, a quick check will reveal that the NPT compliance is determined by the IAEA's Board of Governors, a board made up of thirty-five states, including Russia, China, Venezuela, Mongolia and Cuba.

Now, to be fair to the NPR, there is a caveat. And that caveat is someone has to be fulfilling their obligations in general under nuclear disarmament. It's unclear what they are. And the reason I raise this is not a criticism of the administration, or my friends in the administration of which I have quite a few. But it is to raise this as the issue the Senate is going to be concerned with, and the House of Representatives is going to be concerned with, in dealing with the budgets that are going to fulfill the NPR and the START treaty.

The third issue is some people think numbers don't matter. As General Klotz, the head of Global Strike Command, wrote in a paper for the Air Force Association, I think in December or January, numbers do matter. And Jim Miller, who is the Deputy Undersecretary of Defense for Policy, who is speaking at my seminar series next Thursday, said, again in the paper today, that while the two arsenals—talking about Russia and the United States—need not be equal, we still believe that approximate parity is appropriate with respect to, in particular, deployed strategy systems, especially to make sure there aren't misperceptions, misunderstandings, on either side, any sense of advantage or disadvantage. Very, very important issue. Critical. And I'm glad that Jim raised that issue.

The next question, then, is in my mind does arms control have a strong connection to nonproliferation, counter-proliferation, or the absence of proliferation? In Family Security Matters, I just finished seven parts of a ten-part series on Iran. Parts eight, nine and ten have yet to be published, but the first seven are on there. I have an entire eight single-space page paper on the connection between arms control and proliferation. I've been involved in arms control since I went to work for the Reagan Administration in 1981. And I have to tell you that the record is, at best, mixed, and at worst, not very good. For example, we signed the INF treaty, the START-I treaty, and the START-II treaty. And we found in 1991, Saddam Hussein was six months to a year away from a nuclear weapon. We found the Iranians, in hindsight, we now know they started a nuclear weapons program in 1988 or '89. And we know North Korea started at the end of the Cold War a nuclear weapons program in terms of diverting plutonium from their nuclear reactors, and the IAEA said "something's fishy." And that eventually led to the agreed framework in 1995 under the Clinton administration.

So there isn't necessarily a strong correlation between arms control—involving reducing or eliminating strategic nuclear weapons, however necessary and important and good arms control is—and proliferation elsewhere. Especially to what we call rogue states or terrorist rogue states such as Iran and North Korea from either getting nuclear weapons, or in the case of Syria, trying to get nuclear weapons, when they use North Korean technology, Iranian money, and they build a nuclear reactor, and we have to rely on our dear friends, the Israelis, to take it out. Similar to what the Israelis did in Iraq in, I believe it was 1981.

So proliferation is the toughest problem this administration and any administration has, and I don't envy them their job and it's not a criticism to say that it's a tough issue. And that gets to the points that I handed out today.

The claim is we have ended the drift with the Russians. And that's the reset button. The problem is that the Russians are busy making deals with Venezuela to arm them. The Russians are complicit in the Iranian ballistic missile program and their nuclear program. The Russians also are not exactly being good neighbors with respect to our friends in the Ukraine and Georgia.

And with respect to North Korea, my view is that, I think, the administration has bent over backwards in terms of its engagement policy, and reset policy. It's up to Russia and China to step up, to man up, and come up on the front and do what they should have done a long time ago under the terms of the NPT and that is stop assisting Iran and North Korea with building ballistic missiles or nuclear weapons.

I can't say it any simpler than that—as someone who has pushed very hard for the refined oil sanctions bill that's in Congress, who has testified before many state legislatures on divestment, who's talked about Stuart Levy, who I think is a national hero, who should get a Congressional Medal of Freedom because of the work he has done in terms of Treasury taking money away from rogue states and terrorist elements.

As is now clear, if we do to the Iran central bank what we did to the North Korean bank in Macau, we can perhaps help bring down the regime in Iran. And maybe people disagree with me there. I think we can. That, to me, is the test. And not these namby-pamby sanctions that we pass and then we dilute and then, you know, since 1996, we've had the Iran Sanctions Act. But President Clinton, President Bush, and the new President, have not enforced sanctions against either subsidiaries of American companies or foreign companies with respect to that bill. The power is there to do it and yet we haven't done it. And part of that is there are too many people that have vested interests in doing business with Iran.

As one of my Family Security pieces quoted in the headline, from *The Godfather*, "It's not personal. It's just business." We can't afford that anymore in this day and age. This is too serious an issue. And so fundamentally, to wrap up, what does the NPR do? Well, it preserves a triad. Good. It says, we're not going to get rid of no first use, keep our policy ambiguous. Good. We're not going to de-alert. Good. Missile defense is front and center. Good. With a footnote, and this is what I want to end on, Medvedev said, or Lavrov said, yesterday, that the United States has pledged not to improve the capability of or the number of our strategic missile defenses. That to me means defenses against long-range ballistic missiles, not just Russian and Chinese necessarily, but Iranian missiles that can reach the United States or can reach London. That's a 3400-4000+kilometer missile – that is worrisome and the Senate will have deal with it. And so those are the issues that I would say are front and center with respect to the ratification process of the START treaty in the Senate. Thank you.

FRANK GAFFNEY: Peter, thank you very much. Paula DeSutter, as I said, brings much relevant experience to this topic, both from her days at the State Department in several capacities and from her service here on Capitol Hill with the Senate Permanent Select Committee on Intelligence. She affords us a wealth of knowledge about the larger question of nuclear weapons policy and strategy, but also verification and compliance with treaties that seek to govern such activities. Paula, welcome.

PAULA DeSUTTER: First, you know, as those of us who are interested in all of these issues and trying to understand the Obama nuclear policy, the posture review and the new START treaty would recognize, it's been a busy week. And let me just say that among the top benefits that I see from all of this is that it has reduced the amount of time that the networks have spent on Tiger Woods. So we all have to find those silver linings.

Obviously, the Nuclear Posture Review is just out, two days ago. The START treaty signed today, we have some indicators about what's in it, but I don't, as I sit here today, have a copy of it. So the way I wanted to discuss this was to say there are a number of, and I would highlight five, very serious questions that Congress and the American public need to try to find the answers to in the coming months as we address these problems. The first, that Admiral Monroe addressed, was "why Global Zero?" Second, what are the risks and consequences of the new negative security assurances contained in the Nuclear Posture Review? Third, how well will the new START treaty be verified? And we could also talk about verification of other treaties, space policies or space treaties, Fissile Material Cutoff Treaty, and I'll talk a little bit about the challenges of verifying zero. Fourth, what impact will the new START treaty have on missile defense? And I'll address that only briefly. I think Peter's done a good job on that. And finally, the ultimate question that has to be answered is will the policies and these new documents strengthen or weaken the US nuclear deterrent and US national security?

Having worked at the State Department for an extended period of time, I know that one of the things that diplomats like is to make other countries like us and be nice to us. But that isn't always the primary purpose of our policies. And we have to ask: does it strengthen or weaken national security?

So, turning to "why nuclear zero?" One of the reasons that this has been advocated is the idea that the United States needs to take the lead, because it will have an impact on our ability to persuade countries like Iran and North Korea to give up their nuclear weapons programs. So it's a valid question that people need to ask. To what degree can that be true? I would answer that there's virtually no chance that that would happen. But at least that has to be discussed and debated. Also, the nuclear nonproliferation treaty, Article Six, calls for parties of the treaty to pursue negotiations in good faith on effective measures relating to cessation of the nuclear arms race at an early date and to nuclear disarmament and on a treaty on general and complete disarmament, under strict and effective international control. So the context for the Nuclear Weapons States to disarm is in the context of complete and general disarmament under effective control.

Now, is the Obama administration saying by its advocacy and policies in pursuit of Global Zero, that complete and general disarmament is something that is in the offing? I would say probably no, but we ought to ask that question. Do we think that the world is about to disarm completely, not just in terms of nuclear weapons, but every other weapon known to man? Effective verification, verification under international control, of a global zero, would require all nations of the world to give up their national sovereignty. That's just a bottom line. In order to have real confidence you would have to be able to look at every container that could contain a nuclear weapon. Some of those might be fifty gallon drums. And you would have to be able to go everywhere. That kind of verification does not happen in sovereign states. Finally, I would remind people when President Reagan called for the end of nuclear weapons, which he did, he called for the end of nuclear weapons in the context of a robust ballistic missile defense. And it was the missile defense that was supposed to render nuclear weapons impotent and obsolete. And so, again, you get back to the missile defense question.

I was very concerned about the impact of the new negative security assurances. Recall that the negative security assurances first came up during the Clinton administration, but they specifically indicated that it wasn't just going to be solely retaliation for nuclear weapons use. It was held as a possible retaliation for use of biological or chemical weapons. So the question arises about the Nuclear Posture Review, which says the US will not use or threaten to use nuclear weapons against non-nuclear weapons states that are party to the NPT, and in compliance with their nuclear nonproliferation obligations. So the first question is, should they retitle that section "Making the World Safe For Biological Weapons Use?" We've had event after event where people have said this is perhaps the greatest threat facing us, and I would only underscore that. I am glad that the administration exempted North Korea and Iran from that, because they're not in compliance with the NPT. But what are the risks of telling countries like Syria and a significant number of other states with biological weapons programs, but that we have not yet found to be in noncompliance with the NPT, that biological weapons use only will get a conventional response? The problem is that that could very well mean the engagement of US forces on the ground in that country. That is not always the way we want to be able to fight. It is, I would underscore what Peter said, it is very, very difficult to reach compliance judgments with regard to the nonproliferation treaty.

When I started at the State Department in 2002, I actually brought on a couple of sharp lawyers—not to say that the rest of the lawyers at the State Department aren't sharp—but, in any case, I needed my own to try to do this work. It is correct that the IAEA Board of Governors can reach compliance judgments. It is the national responsibility of participant states to do that, but we're the only country in the world who's done it. We are the only country in the world that has reached an independent judgment that Iran has violated the NPT. But even though the United States has been saying for twenty years that we thought they were pursuing a nuclear weapons capability, it wasn't until 2005 that the United States finally reached that judgment. Now, as difficult as it is already to reach noncompliance judgments, the NPR ensures the political pressure against reaching a compliance judgment about the NPT is going to be even greater than it was. Before it was just, "oh, we'll just refer them to the UN Security Council." Now, if you've reached a judgment that a country is in violation of the NPT, you will be saying it is now permissible for the United States to retaliate against that particular country for BW use with a nuclear weapon. You've escalated the consequences of a noncompliance judgment while not necessarily reducing the risk that the biological weapons would be used. I also believe that the negative security assurances probably further incentivize proxy use of biological weapons, meaning a country like Iran, which has an offensive biological weapons program, could well let Hezbollah use biological weapons and yet that wouldn't necessarily trigger the response. I also find misleading the justification for this in the NPR was that these negative security assurances were okay because of the advent of conventional military preeminence by the US, and continued improvements in US missile defense and capabilities to counter and mitigate the effects of CBW. I think a valid question is are we really, right now, preeminent in terms of conventional capabilities? And second, what the heck are they talking about when they say that the United States has these improvements and capabilities to counter and mitigate the effects of CBW? I'm an attentive observer and I don't know what these are. So what are they?

Finally, how well will the START treaty be verified? It's hard to say at this point. The treaty text, and technical annexes where a lot of the monitoring capabilities will be placed are not currently available. We do know that there's a heavy, heavy reliance on national technical means of verification, or NTM. Our satellites are to observe activities, and detect noncompliance with some onsite measures about which I'm not clear. The problem is that the US imagery constellation, or NTM, is in really, really bad shape.

So is this treaty going to be accompanied by the requisite funding increase in intelligence collection necessary to give us the NTM that we ought to have in order to perform this function? The administration said last July that the post-START verification measures were going to be adapted from START, but that these measures were going to be adapted, simplified, and made less costly as appropriate in comparison with the START-I treaty. Thus far, they've just touted that we have verification measures from the START treaty, but without saying what they are. We know, however, that the intent was to make them simpler and less costly and less demanding. But at lower levels of weapons, verification becomes more important, not less. The consequence of cheating can become more significant, not less.

Now, if you have a robust missile defense, you can accept more risk of cheating on offensive agreements. So the question then, again, goes back to, to what degree are we going to emphasize and really push forward robust missile defense and have we given the Russians, by virtue of the treaty, a veto over the deployment of missile defense? It has all the appearances of that. All US intercontinental ballistic missiles are going to be de-MIRVed to one warhead. That's okay with me. I think that that's more stabilizing. But why aren't the Russians called upon to do the same thing? Among other things, if it's stabilizing for us, it would be stabilizing for them. And it would help you with verification. So the verification capabilities will certainly be scrutinized seriously on the Hill prior to Senate advice and consent to ratification.

Finally, the last point I would make on this is that the current Assistant Secretary for Verification and Compliance and Implementation, my successor, was the lead negotiator on the new START treaty. She is the same person who will be required to prepare a report for Congress that says whether or not the treaty is effectively verifiable. Could there be some conflict of interest in that? Now, it is certainly true that if you're the Assistant Secretary and your administration, your president, has gone forward and signed a treaty, it is not your favorite day at work when you have to tell them that it can't be effectively verified. I know. I had to do that on Fissile Material Cutoff Treaty. It's not your best day at work. On the other hand, if that is your sole mission, then you're going to do that. So there are some conflicts. In any case, I'll stop there and if you want to later, we can talk about any of the other treaties that can't be verified.

FRANK GAFFNEY: Something to look forward to. Paula DeSutter, thank you. As always, you've captured a lot of the inside baseball quality of the challenges that we're facing and I think it adds an important dimension to the analysis. Last but certainly not least, we have a distinguished naval officer, a retired four-star admiral who commanded, he was telling me, in his Pacific fleet alone, a navy larger than the one we're likely to have in the years to come. And he did so with distinction, capping some forty years of service to his country. Adm. Lyons has seen the threats of nuclear war up close and personal, as they say, and has understood as well as any how important it is that the deterrence to those threats be kept credible and what it takes for the United States military to ensure that it's doing its part of that job. So Admiral "Ace" Lyons, welcome.

JAMES "ACE" LYONS: Thank you, Frank. Well, now that you've heard all the good points about the treaty let me touch on a few concerns. As an operational commander, my freedom of action was based in part on the confidence I had in the security and reliability of our strategic nuclear underpinnings. Our allies counted on it. And most importantly, our adversaries recognized it and in part, put bounds on what they might do. Further, we were able to get greater contributions from our allies in a given situation because of the secure, strategic umbrella guarantees. If our allies perceive a pullback on our capabilities, it is quite clear Japan and other allies—South Korea, Taiwan—may see a need to develop their own capabilities.

In that sense, I fail to see how this treaty will enhance deterrence or stability. As I said, I have a number of problems with the START treaty. Many have been highlighted already, not the least of which is there is no symmetry in the treaty. What it does do is contribute to the denuclearization of US forces while the rest of the nuclear powers are modernizing theirs. Russia has embarked on an aggressive modernization program to field new weapons. Its strategy has placed increased reliance on its ICBMs and sea-based missile nuclear forces. These missiles most likely will be MIRVed.

The treaty confers real advantage to Russia, the way I see it. No cuts in their missiles, deployed or strategic launchers, where we have to destroy something along the order of several hundred. How all this enhances our security is certainly unclear to me. By 2015, Russia will have upgraded eighty percent of their long-range missiles. Of course, with our financial help. Their several thousand tactical nuclear weapons are not addressed. I consider this a serious flaw. But what concerns me the most is the lack of consideration of what China is doing. Aside from providing assistance to the proliferation of nuclear technology to states like Iran and North Korea, they have gone in to develop a rapid modernization of their own nuclear force structure to include the development of four more nuclear missiles, some of which most likely will be MIRVed. And we also have to consider they have developed fifth-generation aircraft and a strategic bomber. They have built underground submarine pens on Hainan Island with both strategic and conventional attack submarines. They objected, along with Russia, to our missile defense programs while at the same time they've recently demonstrated their own missile defense capability along with an anti-satellite capability. What the treaty will do in the future to our development of a future antiballistic missile capability is unclear at this time.

With their double digit increase for the last several years to their military budget, every weapons system China has developed is targeted against US forces. Their latest anti-ship ballistic missile is specifically targeted against our carrier forces. This is supposed to be an anti-denial or no-go zone weapon. We have the capability to counter that anti-ship ballistic missile. It primarily rests in our newly-developed Zumwalt class destroyer, with over fourteen billion dollars in research and development invested in it. It's stealthy. It can handle any current threat. It has the growth potential and the cooling capability, all of the power necessary to support future weapons systems, lasers, rail guns, X and S-ban radars. In our wisdom, we're building three with no antiballistic missile capability. Instead, what we decided to do—and this is critically important with the new role the Navy has been tasked with in our antiballistic missile capability—is invest in a restart program to build thirty-year-old guided missile Arleigh Burke destroyers which have no growth potential and only the basic antiballistic missile capability.

This is a serious situation. And by the way, there's no cost oversight or capability oversight on this program. Everything is a shell game. And much of the cost of this new program, which is something on the order of three billion dollars and is fourteen months behind schedule now, is being covered under government-furnished equipment. Further, the ballistic missile agency is funding all the software for these upgrades. So I'm not sure any of this will raise the level of comfort with our allies. This is a program, certainly from the standpoint of an antiballistic missile capability, that needs to be changed.

Let me just touch on the hair trigger alert. And much has been made about it. Let me just say we have a very reliable command and control system. It's secure. The procedures are precise. They've been tested and tested and proved to be reliable. I have total confidence that it will be so in the future. Let me conclude by saying there is no Dr. Strangelove out there in the fleet. And with that, Frank, I'll turn it back to you.

FRANK GAFFNEY: Thank you, Admiral, very much. Let me just add one point to the observation that the Admiral made about the implications of the START treaty for missile defense. I think several of us have remarked on this, but I think it needs to be said very directly. The Russians have put us on notice as recently as this morning's press conference that they will regard "any qualitative or quantitative change" to America's missile defense capabilities as a basis for departing from this treaty. I'm not even sure that President Medvedev limited his ultimatum to just "strategic" defenses; I think he simply said "missile defense."

In short, I hope we are now under no illusion that the Russians could simply say they're no longer conforming to this treaty. As several of us have pointed out, with their MIRVed missiles and their hot production lines for both missiles and nuclear weapons, if they have the funding—and that is a big if – but if they have the funding and the will, they could, conceivably, build substantially more nuclear weapons than they're permitted to have under this treaty.

And we might find ourselves in a position where we have neither the missile defenses that we need nor the deterrent capabilities that are appropriate. So with that, let's open it up.

Thank you for your patience in hearing some long, but I think very thoughtful and important interventions from our panel. And when you address yourself to us, would you please identify yourself and your organization, if any, and also if you have somebody whom you would like to have answer your question, direct it to them, please.

QUESTIONER: Thanks to everyone on the panel here. I wanted to just say that the Kremlin issued a statement. Two sentences or three, right before they signed the treaty. Statement: "the treaty between the Russian Federation and the United States on the reduction and limitation of strategic offensive arms signed in Prague can operate and be viable only if the United States of America refrains from developing its missile defense capabilities, quantitatively or qualitatively. Consequently, the exception"--so, it goes on a little bit more. I can e-mail it to you later. It's on the Kremlin's website. So you're exactly right. And they've issued an unequivocal and unqualified statement saying that—

FRANK GAFFNEY: And then the president of Russia said it in the press conference as well. So this wasn't some unauthorized statement that was put out by somebody else.

QUESTIONER: And it's not surprising. I wanted to ask you, Miss DeSutter, will the treaty adequately verify directly the 1,550 warhead number?

And also, to Peter, will it be necessary to reduce the ICBM silo numbers? If so, by what degree? Cause there's a number of senators who have written that they would not like that to happen. And also, to Miss DeSutter again—

FRANK GAFFNEY: This is a MIRVed question.

QUESTIONER: Exactly—in *Newsweek*, the—*Newsweek*, the NPR, said the administration's still working on nuclear targeting directives at a classified level. Do you have any inklings on this? And what might they be? Thank you very much.

PAULA DeSUTTER: This, the second question is pretty easy. I have no idea how this will influence the nuclear targeting.

As to whether or not there will be direct verification of the 1,550 warhead number, my understanding is that there will be some mechanism for reentry vehicle onsite inspection (RVOSI) as there was under the START treaty. In the START treaty, the Russians repeatedly violated those obligations. We'll have to see how effective their RVOSI, see we love acronyms, how effective that is and also you're not going to go to every single missile and do an RVOSI to count how many warheads are deployed. It's at most—it's certainly going to be a sampling approach. So to what degree will that sampling approach give you the kind of confidence about the numbers deployed on each of the warheads? And at this point, I have to mention that apparently, and I don't fully understand this, but apparently there's an agreement to count every strategic nuclear bomber as one warhead. Now I also note that the NPR refers to the US keeping a triad, including nuclear-capable strategic bombers—but doesn't say we're going to keep strategic bombers. And we also know that Prime Minister Putin has called for the development of new strategic bombers for Russia. So how that will count, I just don't know.

PETER HUESSY: Your question about ICBMs is probably, I think, critical to the whole question of stability and the deterrent. But the treaty requires some cut of 188 missiles and/or bombers, deployed and non-deployed, and less than half of that regarding deployed systems. To get from the eight eighty we have now down to seven hundred, you could eliminate randomly ballistic missiles in the three Minuteman fields that are old—they're giving us the silos with the most trouble—and reduce your maintenance costs. I don't know whether we should do that. I mean, this is the one part of the START treaty I have a real problem with.

The Russians are going to go down to five hundred platforms anyway including old SS-18 missiles. We have over eight hundred and eight; as I said, we're going down to seven hundred. That gets dicey because the submarines you could count—not counting two of the submarines in overhaul. That's forty-eight missiles. And I think that will be part of the START treaty. And then you have to take a certain number of B-52s out of the nuclear mission. And that could get you down to within fifty of where you have to be. But my question is, none of this is necessary. If warheads are the things that go boom and deployed warheads are the things that provide both stability and, if too many, instability, the warhead levels are the key. And I could keep all four hundred and fifty Minuteman, they're all going to be de-MIRVed. I've got bulkheads on the new Grand Forks, North Dakota ones, that I have to take off to put on more than one warhead and that would take a year, well, actually three years, to do all hundred and fifty missiles.

So there's no big breakout capability there. And it's the one part of the treaty that I have real problems with, that seven hundred number. The warhead number I don't have a problem with. It is that seven hundred number. That is—the saving grace may be that we don't have to implement this until the end of the treaty, technically. And by that time we will have a plan, hopefully, to replace Minuteman, probably with another service life extension. Because the current missiles go only to 2020 to 2030. And without that, with four hundred and fifty Minutemen out there, no President of the United States has to make a quick decision in a crisis. And that's why they're so valuable. Remember, during the Cold War we thought they were terrible because they were MIRVed. And we worried about Russia using a hundred missiles with a thousand warheads and taking out everything and having all this in reserve. If everything's MIRVed, it goes to Frank's point, we've got the greatest instability in the world. But the Russians, unfortunately, because of money issues, have highly-MIRVed land-based missiles which are on alert about ninety-seven, ninety-eight percent of the time versus their subs, which are about a third of them at sea. So as Paula mentioned, there is—or Ace had mentioned—there is an imbalance in that force structure.

FRANK GAFFNEY: I know Peter has got to go. If anybody has a quick question for him, I would advise you, if not we'll just take whatever questions we can and we'll thank you, Peter, for joining us and for your contribution. I'm sorry, you have a question for Peter? Okay.

FRED CELEC: Fred Celec from the Institute for Defense Analysis. Several of you mentioned that the Russians were going down to whatever level that they negotiated in the treaty, anyway, for economic or technical reasons, and so, in essence, they wanted to bring our level down to their level. Several of you also mentioned that there's a tremendous imbalance in tactical nuclear weapons. We have a few hundred. They have several thousand. Did anybody have a clue as to why this administration took the one piece of leverage that we had off the table in favor of a treaty that didn't benefit us and they were going to anyway?

PETER HUESSY: Fred, let me go back to the Bush administration. Cause I remember when we raised this issue. I remember people such as J. D. Crouch and others would say to me just simply, forget it. The Russians just won't budge. And you could drop an anvil on them and they won't budge. And I know that the point is that maybe we had more leverage here, but no American president has been able to limit them except for Bush 41 where it was a voluntary, reciprocal, unilateral measure. And afterwards, we determined that Gorbachev didn't follow through. Or he may have told his guys to follow through, but they didn't. So who knows the extent to which they reduced their tactical nukes at the end of the Cold War? I see your point, as that was the one piece of leverage we have big time. We didn't use it. I think they wanted an agreement to get the ball rolling on this and the fissile material cutoff and the CTBT and the, you know, this whole panoply of things, so—

FRANK GAFFNEY: You should be very skeptical of anyone who tells you they're going to capture later the stuff that they couldn't get in this treaty—or maybe they didn't even try to get in this treaty—such as limits on tactical nuclear weapons that, as Peter said, the Russians have insistently refused to negotiate away. Some of those weapons, by the way, we have reason to believe, are sitting off the coasts of the United States right now, pointing perhaps at this city, among others, fitted with warheads having the destructive power of the Hiroshima bomb. None of those weapons are counted in New START. But anybody who tells you they'll get them in the next treaty has a bridge they would like to sell you. And I don't think this is a sound basis for national security policy-making. Peter, I know you have to go. Thank you so much for joining us.

QUESTIONER: I would like to ask if you could comment on the notion of strategic stability, the new NPR, vis-a-vis China. Because China has never officially had a policy of mutual balance. So does it have some further implications? Thank you very much.

JAMES "ACE" LYONS: Yeah. Repeat that for me, Frank—

FRANK GAFFNEY: The question as I heard it was, what do you think is the--the sense of the strategic concept, I guess, of the Chinese in the NPR, the Nuclear Posture Review, what is it we are imputing to them in terms of their theories of deterrence and the like?

JAMES "ACE" LYONS: Well, I think that it had to be recognized as expanding capabilities and the modernization of their forces. This is—while the numbers are not great now, I don't see any restraint being imposed on where they're going with their various programs. And to the point, you know, as Frank mentioned, when I had the Pacific fleet, I had 255 ships, seven carriers, fifty-eight submarines, many of which are SSBNs. And when you look at that today where they maybe halve—where we may have in the entire Navy a number Frank just gave me. 213. Somewhere downstream. What China is doing cannot be ignored. I mean, it skews the whole equation. It's the same way in the development of their conventional capabilities. There are anti-ship ballistic missiles, which can be easily converted. The fact that it's designed—all of these programs that they have are designed to go against US forces. What's their objective? Certainly they want total control and dominance out to the first island chain and the second island chain, which includes Guam, by the way. And certainly, we're now seeing much more renewed interest in the Middle East. But more importantly, they have a very aggressive foreign military sales program. They provided Iran with a number of capabilities, not the least of which is a supersonic cruise missile, which they acquired from Russia, which is specifically targeted to go against our Aegis cruisers.

FRANK GAFFNEY: Could I just add to this? It seems to me that the Chinese view of the world is not uppermost in the minds of the Obama administration. It's one of the great ironies of this whole exercise that you keep hearing the president reviling – that may be too strong a word, but not too much—the old Cold War-mindset of those Bush administration people. And how his team is getting beyond that. Yet, at this very moment, the current administration is demonstrating its attachment to the outdated, dual-superpower Cold War paradigm.

This New START treaty is a throwback to the bipolar world and the constructs of, you know, canonical arms control that at the time seemed—at least to some in this country—to be the optimal way to modulate Russian behavior.

Today, China's growing power is an inconvenient fact. Particularly inconvenient to the government is the reality that China is engaged in the kinds of military programs directly aimed at us, point one, and point two that Beijing is taking an unbelievably holistic approach to warfare.

In fact I would commend to you a book entitled *Unrestricted Warfare*, published in 1999 by the People's Liberation Army. Two colonels wrote it. This book describes at great length numerous ways you can destroy the United States—from financial attacks on our economy to terrorism to biological warfare to, of course, nuclear. And we shouldn't forget that the Chinese have actually *threatened* nuclear attacks against this country. Specifically, a top PLA general said Los Angeles would be nuked if we behaved towards Taiwan in a way they didn't like.

President Obama's fixation—and I don't think that's overstating it—his fixation with the pursuit of a nuclear weapons-free world to be achieved primarily via bilateral reductions in US and Russian arms is an approach that essentially leaves out of the equation the Chinese nuclear program. The effect would be to invite the Chinese to build up to whatever levels either our negotiators achieve or, more likely, Russia's economic circumstances dictate. And that, I believe, is not going to make for a more secure world.

PAULA DeSUTTER: Just to build a little on what Frank said. Parity, which is talked about in the NPR, and it says we don't need to have exact parity with Russia, I think that's right. On the other hand, parity is a Cold War concept, and it was developed and discussed primarily in an era when the only significant nuclear stockpiles were Russian—or Soviet—and American. We are now in a situation that's very, very different. And so, the question that the NPR addresses, you know, do we need exact parity with Russia? It's the wrong question. The question is, does the United States need parity—and I would assert superiority—to all of the other countries who can pose, particularly a nuclear threat, but other threats as well, to the safety of the United States and our allies? That's the question. And that means that you can't just look at Russia and China, but you've got to look at Iran and Syria and North Korea, and you've got to be ready for all of those and you've got to address it, not only with offensive capabilities, but defensive as well. So I think that the stability question is—maybe it's too soon to say that we've been made more dangerous. But I think that it isn't too soon to say that they're asking the wrong questions and therefore one has to wonder if they're going to get the right answers.

FRANK GAFFNEY: Could I exercise the prerogative of the chair to pose a question myself to Admiral Monroe? Something you touched on earlier requires a little bit more development. One of the things that is absolutely explicit in the Obama NPR is that we can live, for the foreseeable future—or at least as long as this president is going to be alive—with the nuclear weapons we have.

They have laid out some exotic explanations of the ways in which they're going to try to maintain the deterrent without "replacing" existing weapons with new ones—relying instead on their "refurbishment" and the "reuse" of previously tested components.

Bob, you were in the business of insuring that nuclear weapons worked. And I would just ask you from the point of view of a true expert to assess the probability of success of this approach. Will we be able to provide for the security of the American people—which the president himself, at least as I hear it, now says will require us to maintain a safe, credible and effective nuclear deterrent for the foreseeable future—without any modernization and without any testing? What are the chances?

ROBERT MONROE: Zero. No, seriously. Our nuclear weapons stockpile today is safe, secure, reliable, but not at all effective. It's meaningless in terms of today's threats. Our arsenal consists of high-yield weapons. They were designed initially to destroy cities, and as the Cold War advanced, we changed to counter-force targeting, to destroy missile silos, magazines, missile launchers, air bases, that kind of thing.

Today, the dominant threat is not the launch of the thousands of warheads at the US. It's that rogue states, two in particular, Iran and North Korea, will develop a nuclear weapons production capability, and they'll get the weaponization right, and eventually they'll have some kind of effective weapon, although they'll certainly be primitive compared to ours. But they'll work, and they'll kill millions. And they will then go into production with these.

And in the case of North Korea, if they have a regime anything like they do at present, they'll sell them to anyone wishing to buy them. I don't mean any state wishing to buy them. Any individual wishing to buy them. If it's Iran, they would most probably be willing to give them to Hezbollah or Hamas or al-Qaeda for use. Now, I talked about deterrence earlier. People seem to think that if we have a 400 kiloton nuclear weapon, this will somehow deter the Iranians from continuing their program. What could we threaten them with? That we will detonate it in the middle of Tehran, killing millions of innocent people, including many women and children? Does anyone believe we'd do that?

But if we had highly accurate, low-yield, reduced residual radiation, earth-penetrating weapons, and they had a nuclear facility underground in a mountain, it's a different matter. This is a credible threat! We would never have to use it. They would comply with our wishes. But the Obama Administration's Nuclear Posture Review states: "We will not develop new weapons, we reject that."

So the word "effective" is a key word. Our current stockpile of nuclear weapons is NOT effective against our principal adversaries! We could probably keep life-extending our overage weapons, if we used all three options that the Strategic Posture Commission of Schlesinger and Perry recommended (reuse, refurbishment, and replacement). But they would not be effective, and they would have no deterrent power. As Frank said, there's just no hope.

FRANK GAFFNEY: Let me see if we can take a question, Bob. But the thing that I really wanted to get at is can you do all of that without nuclear testing to ensure that what you've got actually works even if the weapon is properly designed.

ROBERT MONROE: Two aspects. First, our existing overage weapons. If we go into the reuse, refurbishment, replacement programs, we could probably count on them for a few years without testing, but not for decades. Imagine having, in your community, a fire engine that you were depending on to save your home, maybe your neighbor's home. But it was never started. The firemen never turned the ignition switch. They never fired up the engine, never ran the generator, never did anything. And the fire engine just sat there for five, ten, fifteen, twenty years. Those weapons have been sitting there now for more than twenty years, which was their design lifetime, and they're not inert.

Think of them as physics experiments, cooking away, changing the nature of the components in ways that nobody has any idea. The only way—the only way—these can be considered reliable is with underground nuclear testing. The computer simulations aren't going to tell you a thing, because we didn't know about those conditions—the cracked epoxy, or the change in thickness of a membrane. We didn't know about those conditions when we were in the testing world, so we didn't have any chance to test them.

Second, as regards new weapons we need, the ones that would give us modern-day deterrence, that would deter the real threats today, these have to be tested, because we we've never built or tested weapons like this. There isn't a battery of test data sitting out there in the Nevada Test Site.

FRANK GAFFNEY: So we've got trouble at the very least, and I just—the point I really wanted to emphasize is we're being told that these kinds of workarounds can keep this nuclear enterprise going, essentially indefinitely. And the one thing that I just wanted to underscore from what Bob has said here is especially when you're saying to the people you hope will do that for you under these exceedingly difficult, technically problematic circumstances, you really don't value what they're doing. In fact, you think it's a kind of loathsome activity. Do you really think you're going to have the best and the brightest doing what is arguably the most important work necessary? We're almost--we're actually past time, so I see two more questions here—let me ask you guys to identify yourselves and pose the questions and then we'll answer them and wrap up. Yes, ma'am?

QUESTIONER: Pam Benson from CNN. How important is this strategic triad and what happens to it if there are even further cuts as the administration would like?

FRANK GAFFNEY: I'll take a cut at that. Why do we have a strategic "Triad"? We developed it over many years because each of the legs of the Triad, as they're called—the ground-based missile systems, Peter was talking about, and their silos; the sea-launched ballistic missiles and the submarines that Ace used to command; and the manned bombers – each have unique attributes that are both strengths and weaknesses. And the reason that we believed it necessary to invest enormous amounts of money over many years to develop and deploy these different capabilities was a quite sensible concern that you don't want someone with a breakthrough in anti-submarine warfare to essentially take down your deterrent. Or by bringing to bear breakthroughs in radar technology that keep your bombers from being able to get to their targets.

The trouble is whether you can maintain a viable Triad for the foreseeable future once you get to the low levels of delivery vehicles called for in START. Peter says he hopes it will take seven years before we actually implement all those cuts, providing time to mitigate this problem. I am skeptical.

After all, we have an administration that wants to drive us toward the end of nuclear weapons. Even the previous administration which had no such ambitions implemented ahead of schedule the cuts called for in the strategic arms treaty that Paula was involved with, the Moscow Treaty. And I think that's what should be expected to happen in this case, too—if not on the Russian side, on our side.

But the point I'm making is that we could have a problem maintaining a Triad, either way—and particularly if we go to another round of reductions (to which it remains to be seen whether the Russians would agree). Another factor may be that we are obliged to abandon this balanced strategic posture because our forces are obsolete and unsustainable. Whatever the cause, eliminating one of the Triad's "legs" will expose our forces and our country to risks that we have heretofore decided we could not safely entertain.

JAMES "ACE" LYONS: Increasing destabilization. You're not enhancing anything. I mean, it's that simple.

FRANK GAFFNEY: Well, you may be enhancing the prospects for war. Yes, sir?

QUESTIONER: Everett Gillens here with ZDF German television. I'd like to look into the future with you a little bit. Next week, the summit's coming up. What kind of message do you think the Obama administration is going to send to the world and what kind of message would you rather they send?

FRANK GAFFNEY: Any concluding thoughts on this? The question concerns the meeting next week of the forty-seven, I think it is, heads of state coming together to agree, if the administration has its way, on locking down nuclear materials within the next four years. What do we expect? What would we like to see? Any thoughts on that? Paula?

PAULA DeSUTTER: Well, we know what message they're going to send. The message they're going to try to send is, look, the United States is disarming, we have this agreement with the Russians, and so therefore maybe others could join us in having decent sanctions against Iran, etc. What message do I wish they were sending? I think that even countries that have criticized the United States because of our nuclear weapons, and our reliance on nuclear deterrence, also do enjoy the US nuclear umbrella.

And so oftentimes there are public statements about wanting the United States to disarm, but when pushed and shoved, the reality is other nations want to be able to rely on the US nuclear umbrella. I think that as our numbers go down there is a very real risk that we will be providing increased incentive for other countries that may have wanted a very small number of nuclear weapons for their power or deterrence may now start to see it as we can become real peer competitors, in a nuclear sense, of the United States. As that happens, as missile defenses are constrained because of fears of a veto by the Russians, our missile defense umbrella will be reduced beyond where it is now and I think that that makes things riskier, and the collective security approaches that the United States has advocated for so long, including a viable nonproliferation treaty, including missile defenses and the urging of other nations not to pursue their own nuclear weapons capability because they were covered by ours, I think all of that is at risk. But there will be a lot of celebrations and a lot of press releases and a lot of, you know, "isn't it nice now that the world is all going to be kind to one another?"

FRANK GAFFNEY: I want to conclude by just saying you've heard some scenarios here today that are surely provocative, controversial, and perhaps, to some people's way of thinking, outlandish. We all may or may not agree with one or more of these scenarios or whether they are realistic. For example, I am not certain that there are many countries other than the Chinese who are serious about being "peer competitors," if not actually superior, to the United States in terms of nuclear and other military capabilities.

But the point is that what we are really talking about is what used to be called "thinking about the unthinkable." As a nation we have, for at least a generation now, mostly decided we don't need to do that. Or that we can entrust to a few of us the responsibility for doing so, and the rest of the American people can simply ignore these sorts of issues. And more to the point, they can ignore the fact that there are people elsewhere—whether they are in the Kremlin, in Beijing, in Tehran, in Pyongyang or, I don't know, in Venezuela—that are thinking the unthinkable in ways that will be very detrimental to our well-being and that of others.

And so what we're encouraging here, I hope, is a conversation with the American people about these most important issues. To engage them in a way that we hope will end this sort of illusion that it's either of no interest or somebody else's business to think about what it takes to protect this country in a world that is going to have more nuclear weapons in it—notwithstanding the president's vision—that is going to have more ballistic missiles with which to deliver those weapons, and probably more cruise missiles and perhaps other platforms. Worse yet, more and more of those weapons in the future will probably be in the hands of countries that are hostile to us.

Finally, as Paula's answer suggests, we're going to find ourselves with a lot of countries that, at least in the past, we used to think of allies who decide they have to look to their own security and get their own defenses. A number of them may, as a result, acquire nuclear weapons and be less friendly.

My closing thought to you is most of what we've talked about here today is important in its own right, but it's particularly worrying in the larger context of the doctrine that I think is emerging as that of the Obama administration. I characterize it as the Obama Doctrine: Undermine our allies, embolden our enemies, and diminish our country.

The result will ineluctably be a lot more enemies and a lot fewer allies. And a perception that this is a country that can be, if not attacked with impunity, certainly disregarded in pursuit of aggressive ambitions. That's not the kind of world I think any of us want to live in. And I encourage all of you to take to heart this message and, to the extent you can, disseminate it. By so doing, you will help the nation have the kind of debate we must have, at long last, about where we're going, both with respect to our nuclear weapons policy and our national security policy more generally. With that, thank you very much for coming.

JAMES "ACE" LYONS: One point more. Peter, at the end of his remarks made a comment about how he thought sanctions would work against Iran. He knows my view. I think sanctions are a copout and if you're going to get a handle on the Iranian nuclear threat, we're going to have to do a military strike. ▪

www.ingramcontent.com/pod-product-compliance
Lightning Source LLC
Chambersburg PA
CBHW022125280326
41933CB00007B/555